from nature to plate

THE
KITCHIN®

from nature to plate

Tom Kitchin

Text by Michaela Kitchin
Photography by Marc Millar

WEIDENFELD & NICOLSON

Summer   Autumn

Contents

Sharing my world

'From Nature to plate' is my motto, and it sums up a great part of my life. Nature is life; life is food.

In this book I want to share some of my experiences, as well as my thoughts on the people who inspire me and on the extraordinary produce we have in this country. I also want to help you create simple but delicious dishes using methods I have picked up while working with some true master chefs. I want to give you an insight into my world – into my passion for my ingredients and my love for the seasons.

The recipes I have put together here are a collection of carefully selected dishes that I enjoy making. Some are dedicated to the more advanced cook, but I firmly believe that anyone who loves cooking will gain confidence simply by trying something new. Cooking is all about following the seasons and looking at nature's own matches for the perfect taste combinations. You need to know the basics, but by allowing yourself to discover new techniques and, more importantly, mastering your own palate, you will soon be on to good things.

I spent 13 years working for some of the best chefs in the world. I have been through hell and back many times in the kitchen and on a few occasions I've seriously doubted my choice of career. Cooking is often glamorised in the media, but I firmly believe there is no success without hard work. Like most chefs, I have had to work ridiculously long hours, but there is something incredibly rewarding about cooking. I believe anyone can cook – you just have to put your mind to it and be determined to succeed.

One of the highlights of my career was the day when my wife and I opened our own restaurant, The Kitchin. I guess I always wanted to have my own place, but many times in my career I wasn't sure if I would ever be able to achieve my goal. It was not until I took a new approach to my cooking, by focusing and absorbing every bit of training that I could, that I felt rewarded and the dream of a restaurant seemed less distant. In this book I have shared my ups and downs, the highs and lows of running my own business, but more than anything my sincere love for cooking and local produce. Many of the techniques I use are French, but my ingredients are Scottish whenever possible. By being true to my roots and most definitely always in season, it's all about *From Nature to Plate*.

I grew up in a small community outside Kinross in the Scottish countryside with my mother, father, younger sister, lots of dogs and a donkey – Charlie. As a young teenager I worked as a strawberry picker in the school holidays and then packing broccoli on a local farm, but then one summer I found a job in the local pub, The Lomond Country Inn, washing pots and pans. I liked it from the moment I stepped in the door. I remember my excitement when I first heard the kitchen buzz during service and the shouting – although it was nothing compared to what I was later to experience. I loved it! The kitchen was run by a young chef called Steven Adair, who certainly influenced me and made me start thinking of cooking as a proper job, not just something to pass the time during the summer.

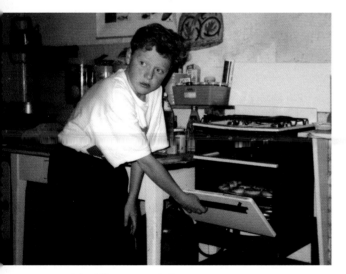

A budding young chef – age ten.

I didn't enjoy school, except for sport and home economics, and at 13 I knew I wanted to be a chef. I was still working weekends and holidays at the pub and I was much happier sitting out in the shed plucking game birds than studying for exams. I couldn't understand the point of staying at school any longer, so at 16, with my parents' approval, I decided to leave and train as a chef.

I was accepted at the cooking college in Perth and spent two years there learning the basics. I was still working part-time at the Lomond and the owner, Mr Adams, noticed my eagerness and ambition and believed I had the potential to become a good cook. When I was nearly 18, he arranged for me to do an internship at Gleneagles, where he had previously been a director. This was a real stepping-stone. I was off to the grand Gleneagles Hotel – a truly spectacular place. For me, it was a totally new experience and the first time away from home.

My first few months at the hotel were hard. At that time there were 70 chefs in the kitchen and everything was made from scratch. Beautiful local produce would arrive every day and it was a tough job to butcher, fillet and prepare everything in time for service. My friend and fellow chef Dominic Jack and I used to sit in his small room in the evening after service reading about Marco Pierre White, Pierre Koffmann, Michel Perraud, Raymond Blanc and Michel Roux and we felt inspired by them. We used to read their books, talk recipes and ideas, and dream about one day meeting those chefs – or even possibly working for them. We were pretty comfortable in our little world up at the hotel, but we also knew that the next step, and the only way of getting any further in our careers, would be to get in touch with these greats. We wanted them to teach us to become better chefs. It was an exciting time and Dominic and I shared the same grand plans.

Dominic and I in the kitchen at Gleneagles, 1995.

Dominic left Gleneagles to work with Michel Perraud at Fleur de Sel in Sussex and I talked with my senior sous-chef, Gibby, about my next move. I wanted to work in or near London. Gibby encouraged me to contact Le Manoir aux Quat' Saisons, Le Gavroche and La Tante Claire and with his help I got the chance to do a *stage* – a trial day working for free with the possibility of getting a job – at La Tante Claire for Pierre Koffmann.

When I knocked on the famous La Tante Claire door in Royal Hospital Road I was excited about meeting Koffmann, the enormous Frenchman. Thinking I was already a chef, I had my knife box under my arm and a bag on my shoulder; I was wearing my new Levi's jeans and my hair was tied back in a ponytail. Pierre Koffmann took one look at me, mentioned something about my hair in his strong French accent and told me to get changed. Shortly afterwards he put me in the corner peeling potatoes, which is where I spent most of the day. I secretly watched Pierre Koffmann from where I stood – he was cooking, swearing, sweating, chopping and in full action every minute of the day. I immediately wanted to be part of it all. I couldn't quite believe what I saw – or heard. Mr Koffmann stood shouting out orders, running his kitchen like an army – his

presence in the kitchen was immense. I had heard so much about him and it seemed amazing to me that this was the same guy – the toughest chef, a master. I also remember thinking he was a lot more human than I had ever imagined.

Koffmann told me I could start work the following week. I accepted and there was no turning back. I guess what sold it to me was that I was going to have the opportunity of working alongside Chef himself – the legend of cooking and one of the most famous chefs in the UK. Little did I know then that he was to become like a second father to me. From the start, Koffmann inspired me like no one else ever has in my life and he stood out to me as the greatest chef. He has never to this day failed to impress me. I will admit that working for him was one of the hardest, most gruelling things I've ever experienced, but at the same time it was the best school I could have attended. Many times during my years with Koffmann, I felt completely and utterly exhausted and broken, but I honestly believe that had I not done those years with him I would not be the chef I am today.

What I especially admire about Koffmann is how he cooks from the heart. He is strong and confident in his skills and he doesn't care what anyone else thinks about how he runs his kitchen or how he relies on his palate. He has an amazing appreciation of food and a remarkable understanding of flavours and how to combine them. Frankly, his knowledge of food and produce stretches beyond that of anyone I have ever worked with, and my respect for Koffmann is now for so much more than just cooking.

If I say that my first week was a week in hell, I am not exaggerating. I went to hell and back. And *quickly!* After my first week in the job I was in serious doubt about my cooking skills and everything I had ever learnt. My confidence sank with every day that passed, and I wondered if I could even put the stove on. But of course I wasn't even allowed anywhere near the stoves in those early days. I had to pick herbs and chop vegetables in the back, which I was secretly quite happy to do. I was safe from the carnage of the kitchen as I hid in my corner and it slowly dawned on me that I had been very naive. I knew from the age of 13 that I wanted to be a chef, but I soon realised that working as a chef in a busy prestigious London restaurant is many miles away from the quiet cosiness of a country pub in Scotland. Not to mention the fact that I was working for Koffmann. Although I was young, I knew of some of the famous chefs who had been though his kitchen – Marco Pierre White, Gordon Ramsay, Eric Chavot, Tom Aikens, to name just a few.

I pushed myself from morning until night, treating every day as if it was my last. After my first week at La Tante Claire, I was put on the starter section. I spent more than four months there, with my eyes set on progressing to the veg section. We worked from 7am to midnight, five days a week, and the afternoon break, if only 30 minutes, seemed essential for survival. Then one day, Koffmann decided I was to walk his dogs.

Every other day for three months I had to walk Chef's dogs in my afternoon break. One of the dogs, Bobo, was so old and slow I was absolutely petrified he would collapse and die on me as we strolled down Royal Hospital Road towards Battersea Bridge. Luckily this never happened and I learnt to use the dog walks to think about the afternoon ahead and mentally prepare myself for service. I was pretty scared of Koffmann, but at the same time totally in awe of him. I was especially impressed by his 'no waste' policy. Nothing goes to waste in Koffmann's kitchen. Absolutely nothing. This has been one of the many things I have learned from him. Nothing will ever go to waste in my kitchen.

As the days went by I picked up new skills and I had an enormous hunger for learning new techniques in order to master my craft. After my months on the starter session I was moved to the veg section. That was a big step for me and with it came a lot of new responsibility. I survived for two months and managed to get everything ready on time and do what was expected of me. Koffmann cooked the meat during every service, and I put the garnish on the plate. God, it was hard, but I thought I was doing all right.

But one day I came into work to find that someone else had been given my job and I was back on the starter section. I was not happy. The new boy was some cocky guy from the kitchens at the Connaught. He was full of confidence and everything about him annoyed me instantly. However, the new arrangement didn't last long. The guy's confidence slowly started to disappear and I could tell that he was struggling. After three weeks in his new role, he didn't show up one day after the lunch break. I was put back on the veg and this time I was not going to give it up for anything. I had secretly built up my confidence in the Tante Claire kitchen and I started to feel that I had guys under me who were going through a bigger hell than I was.

I had my allies – my friends Helena Puolakka from Finland and Raphael Duntoye. Both have an enormous talent for cooking that you find in only a few people and Koffmann saw their potential. We always had a laugh together when Chef wasn't around and I sometimes think to myself that if it hadn't been for Helena and Raf I would not be sitting here now. They were my life-savers at times – and they know it. They've both gone on to do great things. Helena is heading up the Skylon restaurant at London's Royal Festival Hall, and Raphael is at La

Petite Maison in Mayfair, which is one of my all-time favourite restaurants,

Then came the day when my career as a chef nearly ended. The person on the veg did the staff food at Tante Claire. That was me. The staff lunch was served at 11.30 sharp and as I put the food out, I noticed Koffmann disappearing to the fridge downstairs. Shortly afterwards, he shouted my name and I could tell from the tone of his voice that I was in trouble. Koffmann had found some potato trimmings in the fridge, which I should have used for the staff lunch. He was not happy and before I had a chance to speak, he threw the whole bucket of potato trimmings, water and all, straight at me. As the food I had prepared wasn't quite enough for all the staff to be fed, Chef then headed straight to my fridge and took out all the mis-en-place I had been preparing since 7am that morning – all my veg, all my garnishes – and gave them to the staff to eat. I was left with nothing. The first guests were due at 12.30 and I was in deep trouble.

That is when I felt that I'd had enough. I was tired beyond belief and simply could not do any more. I felt I could not last another day. Why on earth was I putting up with this? What was the point? No way was I going to get all my mis-en-place ready before lunch. It was impossible. I packed my knives and my jackets, while trying to fight the tears that were building up inside. I was heading for the door when Helena pinned me against the wall and said, 'What the hell are you doing? You're just having a bad day and you're going to spoil everything you've worked for by walking away! You must stay and fight it!'

Well... I stayed. Her words were ringing in my ears for days and probably years to come. Was I about to throw everything away just because of one bad day? Surely not. But there were so many bad days and I

La Tante Claire, Royal Hospital Road, London, 1997.

could never see an end to it. I still see this incident as one of those defining moments in my career. I was so close to leaving it all, but am I relieved that Helena was there to make me stay! It's all credit to her that my cooking career didn't end there and then. Helena stepped in and gave me a helping hand and we managed to get all the mis-en-place and garnish ready with just about a minute to spare before lunch. I know now that Koffmann was teaching me a lesson – and, boy, did he. No way was he going to jeopardise his standards by me not being ready on time, but that did not even cross my mind as I was rushing to get it all ready. He obviously knew what could be achieved under a bit of pressure.

After a year on the veg section I was totally into my new role. I worked fast and I was comfortable in my

ability to do the task. Chef then decided to put me on the fish section and I struggled every single day. One day I cracked and told him I just couldn't do it. Koffmann must have seen the look in my eyes and for the first time ever he took me outside for a talk. He told me to keep going, and he said that I had potential and he believed in me. I couldn't believe that these words came from Koffmann and although exhausted, I pushed myself once again.

Koffmann decided to join me on my section and I was desperate not to mess things up in front of him. I did all the jobs, but most days I decided to leave the expensive fish, the wild sea bass and turbot, for Koffmann to do, as I was scared of doing something wrong. One day Chef asked me if I was avoiding the sea bass – I was, of course, but didn't want to say so. He told me to get on with it so I took my knife and cut through the fish's belly. All hell broke loose.

'Never ever cut a sea bass in the stomach!' the Frenchman shouted. 'The knife needs to go up and over the ribcage and the belly must be attached to the main fillet.'

Soon afterwards, Koffmann left seven expensive sea bass in my fridge and went out for a meeting, which I knew would last until lunchtime. I had two options – leave them or get on with it. I filleted all seven, just the way Chef had told me, and when he returned he looked at them and said nothing. I knew this was a good sign. I know he was just waiting to see if I had the balls to do them. Koffmann stepped away from the fish section that day and left me on my own. My confidence grew.

Many times since opening my own restaurant I have thought about those hard days during my Koffmann years and often I have been faced with young chefs in my own kitchen breaking down and telling me they can do no more. It's always difficult being put under pressure in the kitchen, especially when tiredness gets the better of you, but I always tell young chefs to stick it out if I believe they have talent. I could never push anyone into being a chef if they don't have the ambition or the drive to be one. Being a chef is a whole way of life and it certainly isn't easy, or terribly sociable, but it's down to you to get on with the job, or get out. I believe that you can tell good chefs within minutes of watching them work, by observing how they clean the stove and how they sweep the floor, as well as how they look at you, the chef. It's well known that some of the best chefs in the world started as pot washers, as this gives them the chance to observe the kitchen from a distance. They get to live the kitchen buzz without being in the middle of the heat. At La Tante Claire, Barry, the kitchen porter, was so good at washing pots and pans that Chef encouraged him to start making the bread for the restaurant. He turned out to be one of the best bread makers who ever went through Koffmann's kitchen.

My social life during my years in La Tante Claire was pretty limited. As my wages were not the best and we were closed every Saturday and Sunday, I used to pick up extra work on my days off so I could at least afford to have a few drinks on Sunday night with friends. It was pretty crazy, and I was exhausted but it was my life and I loved it. My flatmate worked for Anton Mosimann's party service and I sometimes did a few hours for him to help out. This is how I met my future wife Michaela – although I had no idea she was later to be my wife when I first met her. She thought I was arrogant and I probably was. Michaela and I became close friends, although it was not until seven years later that this became a romance. Michaela was busy building her career and I was madly in love – with cooking! Cooking was what kept me going and nothing was going to get in my way.

Sharing my world

In the autumn of 1998, Koffmann told me the restaurant was moving premises to The Berkeley, at the corner of Piccadilly and Berkeley Street in Knightsbridge. The new owner of the Royal Hospital Road premises, Gordon Ramsay, an old Koffmann protégé himself, paid frequent visits to Mr Koffmann during the period of negotiations and take-over and, possibly because we're both Scots, we were soon introduced. Already I could sense that Gordon Ramsay was on to big things. I knew how hard his kitchen was, as some of the guys I worked with had come from there. Gordon was young and ambitious and probably one of the most talked-about chefs in London at the time, being at the height of his success at Aubergine, his restaurant in Chelsea.

One thing I noticed, though, when observing Gordon and Koffmann having their coffee, was the enormous respect Gordon always showed Koffmann. Both came across as so natural and 'human' outside their kitchens. In their kitchen environments I knew that they were both incredibly demanding to work for and both were known for their discipline and great organisational skills. Chefs in their league need to be perfectionists and it was almost impossible for anyone, especially a youngster like myself at the time, to imagine the high level of concentration required to run busy kitchens like theirs.

Working in a restaurant can easily make anyone a bit mad at times. In later years, I have seen the same trait in many chefs, myself included. The pressure of a busy kitchen can turn the best of us into quite different characters while in the heat of a busy service.

I was worried about where my money would come from if we were to close while moving premises, but Koffmann had already taken care of that. He arranged a month's work for me at the famous Le Gavroche under the Roux brothers, followed by another month at Chez Nico with Nico Ladenis. Working at Le Gavroche was a dream come true. I was told to come in for 6.30am on my first day. I didn't want to be late so I showed up at 6.15am on the Monday morning to find the kitchen already buzzing. All the chefs were there. All the boys were working away, heads down, nobody talking. Just like La Tante Claire. I instantly felt at home, did my job and observed. I started to understand the true family tree of gastronomy. Pierre Koffmann was indeed a Le Gavroche boy. As Head Chef of the Waterside Inn before his La Tante Claire days, he had obviously been enormously inspired by the Roux brothers.

Then I went to Chez Nico, which was a completely different kitchen from those I was used to. It was very interesting and a great experience. The food was of an extremely high standard, but by this time I had started to understand what sort of food I enjoyed and my own style of cooking. I was at Chez Nico for one month and then returned to Koffmann. I was intrigued though, as I realised that everywhere I turned there was someone who had been through Koffmann's kitchen. The head chef at Chez Nico, Paul Rhodes, was one of them.

I stayed with Koffmann at The Berkeley for another year, but then I felt it was time to move on and try something new. As much as I enjoyed working for Pierre Koffmann and being in his kitchen, it was time to see something different. By this time I had been with Koffmann for two and a half years. I tried to say to Chef that I wanted to leave and work at a new restaurant, soon to be opening, as a sous-chef. It was double the salary and better hours. Koffmann laughed and said, 'You think you're ready to be a sous-chef at 21? Don't be so stupid!' Not long after this he arranged for me to go to Paris.

I was 21 and broke, but with an enormous appetite for cooking. Koffmann sent me to work for Guy Savoy, one of the most respected chefs in Paris. My French was poor and I had no accommodation – just the job – as I arrived in the French capital. I was paid little money, which left me with about £150 to live off for the month. My friend Dominic was also working in Paris so I slept on his kitchen floor, on a terribly uncomfortable lilo, for a full year. Although I was working six days a week from 7am until midnight I loved Paris and everything about it.

Guy Savoy is a man with impeccable knowledge who runs his kitchen like a fine orchestra. He, like Koffmann, had three Michelin stars. Where Koffmann had taught me the real foundations of cooking – the beauty of working with your produce, using every single piece of it, the art of butchering and filleting – and opened so many exciting doors, Guy Savoy was equally exciting with his artistic techniques, his ability for dressing plates and his passion for the art of cooking. My French improved. My salary didn't unfortunately, but I was living food, going to the markets in the morning and talking recipes with Dominic in the evenings. It was a new world and I learnt to appreciate the beauty of local produce from my visits to the markets. The importance of seasonality, which Koffmann had been so passionate about, was there right in front of my own eyes.

Once my year in Paris was up, Koffmann told me to come back to his kitchen and work for him again. I was now promoted to sous-chef. I was excited about my new role of course, but it was tough. The restaurant was open six days a week and while there had been 16 or 17 chefs when we first moved to The Berkeley there were now no more than seven. It was hard work, but I didn't realise how much I had missed

the buzz of being in Koffmann's brigade until I was back. I started on the fish section when I returned, and as soon as a vacancy came up for the meat, I took it on.

For me this was a great challenge, as I had never before been in control of the meat section. In the past, it had always been Chef himself doing the meat; now he was my teacher. It was head-down, from 7am to midnight six days a week and instead of the 40 or 50 covers at the old La Tante Claire, we were now doing 80 or 90 covers a night. I was shattered. I remember thinking at the time that my job was the hardest anyone could possibly have.

I especially remember the game season, when grouse, woodcock, hare and venison all arrived, as one of the outstanding and toughest periods of the year. We had to pluck, butcher and prepare all the produce as it came in and I thought the work would never end. I loved it, and I could see how much enjoyment Chef got from working with the game, but it came with a lot of hard work, skill and devotion.

I think it was during my days at La Tante Claire at The Berkeley that I started to dream about one day having my own restaurant. I wish I could say that a certain situation or moment made me look at things differently, but I think it was just something that grew on me and one day it became clear that this was what I was working towards. I began to look at my job and responsibility in a new way. I guess this was down to my own personal development and I suppose I had matured in the way I dealt with my job. With every task I felt stronger and I was trying to find ways of turning the hard days into a good experience. I never ever told anyone that I wanted to have my own place, but I was quietly absorbing all the new techniques and skills I could, with the aim of one day using these to my own advantage.

Sharing my world

At this point I felt that I had mastered the basics: I knew how to clean a kitchen properly, how to make good stock, how to butcher a whole piece of meat and fillet a fish, and the importance of seasoning. I was still trying to come to grips with the fact that there would always be good days and incredibly hard days in a kitchen, but I had been with Koffmann for more than five years and needed to consider my next move.

I had always been inspired by the great French chefs, especially Michel Bras and Alain Ducasse, and I applied to them both for a job. I went for a week's work experience with Michel Bras and was very impressed by his skills and his use of the produce around him. I was offered a job by him and by Alain Ducasse, but felt more drawn towards Ducasse and his style of cooking. I was also conscious of how much there was to learn when I took the job at Le Louis XV, Ducasse's famous restaurant in Monaco. Life was about to get tougher still.

I arrived in Nice. I was 25 now and pretty confident in my cooking abilities. As I sat on the bus to Monaco

The ultra-pristine kitchen at Le Louis XV, Monaco.

my adrenalin was pumping as I thought about the fact that I had landed a job working with one of the greatest chefs in the world. I was keen to put my skills to the test and work hard to prove myself and be one of his team. As long as I could stay focused, I would be fine. I had read numerous things about Alain Ducasse and his famous restaurant, his style of cooking, his uniqueness of style and his amazing produce, but I wanted to see it all with my own eyes. I arrived and was escorted in through the front door of the grandest hotel I had ever seen, straight to the concierge desk. I was told to take my bags around the corner to the office. I found the door to the restaurant's office and I was met by Vincent Lung, a friendly Frenchman, who showed me to my staff accommodation. My room was small, and I was staying with three other guys. All of us were sleeping in the same room, sharing one bathroom. Welcome to my glamorous new life!

I showed up an hour early on my first day in the kitchen. I wore my short-sleeved chef's whites and my black trousers but was soon told that a short-sleeved chef's jacket was unacceptable. In London, every chef wore any chef jacket and a bib apron – it was the style at the time and perfectly comfortable and acceptable. This kitchen was different. Everyone wore the same style of jacket, all pressed, all perfect, with a neck scarf and hat. It was like the army. I met Franck Cerutti, the chef, who arrived a short while after me. The first thought that entered my mind as he shook my hand was that his hair was curlier than mine. Bizarre, I know. I felt intimidated as he looked me up and down, and I realised I was going to be the odd one out in this kitchen. This was not Guy Savoy, not La Tante Claire – it was a completely new world.

Working here was not going to be an easy ride. I had been a sous-chef at La Tante Claire, second in charge under Koffmann, but a part of me felt that here I was back at my first job again. And I was, almost. Shortly afterwards I was told that my position of third commis was the lowest position in the kitchen. I knew this before I came and had somehow managed to talk myself into thinking it was the best thing that could happen. Nobody had any expectations of me – I would work hard and get on with it and then move up the ladder. The kitchen was full of Frenchmen. I was the first Scottish person ever to work there and was instantly known as L'Ecossais, the Scot, by the other chefs. There were around 25 of us in the kitchen – 25 chefs to serve 50 guests. How was this possible? I soon found out. The fact that all these hands were needed to create the dishes we had to produce was a mind-blowing experience for me.

I was eager to learn and didn't allow myself to break down, but I was pushed to a degree I had never experienced before. The term 'à la minute' suddenly had a new meaning. Everything was done à la minute here; nothing was prepared in advance. As soon as the order was called through, chefs started to prepare vegetables and cook live shellfish. Even pasta and risotto were made to order.

On my first day I noticed how everybody just seemed to get on with their job, paying no attention to a newcomer like me. Only one person bothered to introduce himself – Massimo Pasquarelli, the only Italian in the kitchen. He had worked in New York before joining the Louis XV kitchen and his English was good. We got on well straight away and became great friends. I have never before met anyone of his standard who found cooking so easy. Cooking is just the most natural thing to Massimo and he has my utmost respect to this day.

The Louis XV kitchen was immaculate. The stove shone after every service, every surface was like a

With Chef Franck Cerutti at Le Louis XV, 2002.

mirror and there were separate fridges for each and every vegetable. One of my main jobs was to clean my section – I even had to scrub some parts of the stove with a toothbrush! After my first week, my back was aching so much that I felt as if I had gone through the toughest circuit training. I could hardly lift my right arm. All because of the cleaning.

As a commis chef on the fish section team I also had to gut and scale all the fish. The chef de partie Christophe Martin smirked as he shouted out commands. He pushed me to a degree that I had never experienced before and I soon realised that this was one of the hardest sections. I felt that I was only there to amuse the other chefs to see how long I would last. Christophe hammered me day and night and I had honestly never met anyone like this guy before. He was stony faced and seemed to be out to get me and see me fail. I was shattered, but at the same time I felt incredibly strong and didn't allow myself to get downhearted.

I slowly started to gain respect from the other chefs. I kept on telling myself that I had worked in one of the hardest kitchens in the UK – La Tante Claire – and surely this couldn't be much harder? Although I was the lowest of the low in this kitchen I was not a boy anymore. I was a young man and I knew how to handle myself. I had skills and I wanted to learn more. I stayed on the fish for one year and then moved on to the vegetable section before moving to sauces. It took me years to realise that Christophe Martin was actually a human being and, although I hate to admit it, he's a really nice guy underneath and a truly outstanding chef.

By the end of my two years in Monaco, I was in a serious dilemma about what to do next. I adored working in the South of France and my desire to have my own restaurant was stronger than ever before. I never at this stage doubted that I had an ability to cook, but I worried about the many other things there were to know about running your own restaurant and I didn't know if I was yet up to the task. I suppose I started to doubt my own ability as a restaurateur, as I observed the team behind Ducasse and began to understand the many different jobs, such as PR, personnel, front of house, relationships with suppliers, which were all things that you don't have much time to think about when working in the kitchen. Cooking is just a small part of the big picture and in no way possible without the many other elements I realised were needed.

My dream of a restaurant became more and more distant and I knew I wasn't ready. Frankly, I started to wonder if I ever would be. How could I possibly work 16 hours a day in the kitchen and get involved with the outside world? As much as I tried to catch up with my newspaper in my break, there was a lot more out there that I almost felt I had missed out on. I suppose it is fair to say that by this time I started to focus properly. I started to think ahead, realise my responsibilities and pay attention to other things, as well as my cooking. I had my vision set, yes, but at the same time I felt quite lost not knowing where to turn next. Should I find work in another great kitchen or should I try something else?

In the spring of 2004, I was ready to move on. I wanted more experience, so I got in touch with an agent to talk about my next move. He suggested that I should try my hands at private cooking and he knew that Sir Anthony and Lady Bamford were looking for an executive chef for their yacht, M/Y *Virginian*. I went for an interview with Lady Carole Bamford and discovered that she was as passionate about her

The Bamfords' yacht M/Y Virginian, *2004.*

food as I was about my cooking. I simply couldn't resist the offer she made me of being the chef on their private yacht which meant travelling the Mediterranean, seeing new places and going to the food markets every morning to buy produce. Lady Bamford, I soon discovered, also has a fantastic eye for style and a real flair for arranging dinner parties to suit the season and surroundings. She opened many new doors for me and brought fresh inspiration to my cooking. While I was used to the frenetic life of restaurant kitchens, she helped me to appreciate the importance of simplicity in food and the joy of working with the best local ingredients. She had eaten in all the best restaurants in the world, but would always appreciate simple food, such as a Sunday roast chicken or a freshly made tomato and mozzarella salad in Italy, just as much, if not more at times. In my

On the pier at Château Léoube in the South of France.

early days with the family I found it difficult to adjust to my new world outside the kitchen. I had to slow my pace, reflect on new ideas and discover this new exciting food world that came with being a private chef. I admit that it was hard at times to work for a foodie family like the Bamfords, as they knew exactly what they liked to eat and how they liked it, but I was making the most of it and after the first few weeks I absolutely loved the job. Lady Bamford's right-hand man, John Hardwick, gave me a great deal of support and helped me to understand what the family was expecting from me.

I was used to the procedure of a busy kitchen – the mis-en-place, service, doing up to 50 covers in two hours – and I now had to adjust to my new world of cooking meals for anything between two and 50 people. It was a totally new experience but I soon learnt to expect the unexpected. I now had to adjust to my employer and their guests in a completely different way than before. I had to plan my food purchases, ensure I could get the very best produce no matter where I was and be flexible with the timings for dinner or the number of guests.

I was also facing new challenges, such as cooking basic dishes. As part of my job I was expected to produce shepherd's pie, omelette Arnold Bennett and other traditional British recipes. Some of these dishes, I hadn't cooked since college and I was not always sure I was getting them right. I had to go back to basics, read new books on British cooking and explore the internet for ideas for family food, but it was a buzz for me. It was so different from what I was used to, but once again I started to appreciate other types of food and dishes than those I would normally cook in a restaurant.

As the yacht cruised through the Med, I got to know all the local markets and found it incredibly

At Club 55, just before proposing to Michaela.

thrilling to discover the different produce in each area. I used to love speaking to the people behind the stands, getting to know their stories and sharing their passion for their home-grown produce. Some of the produce just blew me away and on many occasions I've explored the food markets of southern France and Italy while making up dishes in my mind and experimenting with food ideas. Visiting the food markets with Lady Bamford was a great experience and she watched me as I was negotiating good prices for produce. She was incredibly encouraging and interested in what I was doing, and through her and Sir Anthony I was introduced to some wonderful people. Many shared my passion for food and its origins, and some would later visit me at The Kitchin.

During my time with the Bamfords I saw some amazing places and I spent some time in Barbados cooking with the locals and picking up new ideas for dishes. I also worked with Lady Bamford at her business, Daylesford Organics in the Cotswolds, which inspired me enormously. I loved the quality of the ingredients, the excitement of using produce grown in the vegetable garden and meat from the animals on the estate.

In June 2005 I proposed to Michaela. She accepted, as I bent down on one knee during a busy Sunday lunch at Club 55, the beach club in St Tropez. Looking back, I guess that a proposal over a good meal and some delicious wine was just the most obvious and romantic setting. I had known Michaela for many years and we had a strong friendship. She

Sharing my world

had visited me in France and Monaco and she was an important person in my life during all the years of hard training. We even shared a flat for a few years as friends while she was training with The Savoy and I was at La Tante Claire. Then, one evening, over a magic dinner in Dubai, we both fell head over heels in love and it changed our lives completely. Michaela was based in Dubai at the time, working at the super-luxury hotel Burj Al Arab as business development manager, and like me, she had spent 12 years building her career, in her case in catering and hotel management. The moment we fell in love I knew she was the one for me, and luckily she felt the same.

Michaela and I decided to move back to London for a while, as we wanted to spend time together, and by then we were talking seriously about the possibility of opening our own restaurant. I had been speaking with Pierre Koffmann, my former chef and mentor, about doing something with him. He had sold his beloved La Tante Claire and was playing with the idea of opening something new. I was more than excited about the prospect of opening a restaurant with Pierre Koffmann, but was also determined to do my own thing. Michaela and I didn't have much experience in setting up a business – I certainly didn't. Michaela possessed many qualities and had experience in sales, PR, marketing and front of house, which I didn't, but with our different skills we complemented each other and we were always convinced of our strength as a team. For me, there was nobody more suitable as a business partner than Michaela and there was nobody who knew me or could handle me like she could. We both had fantastic CVs, having worked with some of the best in the business, but above all we shared an enormous ambition to succeed and a sincere passion for the

hospitality industry. We both knew what hard work was – there was no question about that.

We moved to Scotland on 2 January 2006 with the aim of realising our dream and, with help and encouragement from my dad, we started writing our business plan. My dad Ron has been a businessman in Edinburgh for many years and has not only an enormous network of contacts in Scotland but also a lot of experience in setting up businesses and mentoring work with The Prince's Trust. Dad guided us through the early days and has remained a major influence in the business. One of his many pieces of advice right from the start was to approach at least three different companies from each sector to gain a full understanding of what we were after and to find the right people to be part of our plans. We listened to his advice and have used this same method ever since. Our aim was to create a restaurant that would bring a new concept to Edinburgh's dining scene. Our ideas were simple: provide great, affordable food, in stylish welcoming surroundings with customer service to match. In February 2006 we founded the company – The Kitchin LLP (what else could you call it with such a surname!). Over the next few months we worked day and night trying to achieve our target of opening that June.

We did an enormous amount of research on the Edinburgh dining scene, as we desperately tried to find a property we could afford. We eventually found a place in Leith on Commercial Quay. It was known as the 'graveyard of restaurants' as four restaurants had come and gone in the previous five years but we liked it – and after negotiation we could just about afford the lease. The property was a converted warehouse in the heart of Leith, the old port and docks area of Edinburgh. The setting for the film *Trainspotting*, this was once an area that people used to avoid due to its many problems with drink, drugs and prostitution, but things had changed. We instantly felt that the place had charm and character and we liked the funkiness of Leith. After much research and with a limited budget we settled for the Commercial Quay property.

It was always obvious that Michaela would take on the role of general manager. Her hands-on approach and work ethic is the same as mine and her great knowledge of all aspects of hospitality left her in charge of the day-to-day running of the restaurant and email correspondence, not to mention the enormous amount of office work. Although Michaela was working day and night on the computer (and still is), she was adamant that she wanted to meet and greet all our guests to add that touch of personal service to the restaurant. I was of course delighted for Michaela to look after our guests, as her ability to provide service is second to none. Michaela has

The day before the opening of The Kitchin.

Opening day of The Kitchin, 3 June 2006.

always stressed the importance of service and offering a non-intrusive welcome to our diners, and this has indeed proved to be successful. I suppose it was not until I saw her interacting with our guests, and heard some wonderful comments from them after a meal, that it fully sank in that service is as important as the meal itself. A good meal will never be perfect if not matched by the service and we have certainly made a point in sticking to this concept since and insist on all our staff keeping to it.

As the business started to take shape, we soon realised we needed a bookkeeper. The huge amount of paperwork and invoicing involved in running a restaurant was something we had not fully appreciated. Nobody ever teaches you those aspects of having your own business when you train as a young chef, that's for sure, and we had to learn about VAT and other daunting expenses, which we had not fully accounted for in our projections. We also started a two-year, day-to-day cash flow projection to ensure we were always in total control of our finances. This is still in place today, updated every morning with the previous day's takings, and has certainly proved its worth in helping us to forecast financial fluctuations.

The next months were filled with meetings, day and night. We met with shopfitters, plumbers, upholstery companies, interior designers, graphic designers, furniture companies, licensing boards, electricians, solicitors, painters, kitchen fitters – at least three from each sector – and we found wonderful people with similar passions to our own. I know now that some of these people did us a favour because they believed in us and we are incredibly grateful. My dad always used to say, 'You're only as strong as your weakest link', and we still apply this rule. Every member of our team is vital, due to his or her expertise in a particular field. A strong team remains one of our hallmarks. We would only ever employ people who share our vision and passion for making our business stronger.

And then there are our suppliers. In the early days when we had just returned to Scotland, Michaela and I travelled around the country meeting some outstanding people. Our aim was always to provide our diners with seasonal, local food, and with the help of our graphic design team, Contagious Design, we developed our 'From Nature to Plate' philosophy and brand. We also introduced ourselves to the many chefs and restaurateurs of Edinburgh – Martin Wishart and Andrew Fairlie were particularly helpful.

Michaela took charge of the interior design of the restaurant. We had limited funds and had to spend most of our budget on buying the right stove and fittings for the kitchen. Michaela insisted on keeping the old stone features of the building and by matching these with grey tones throughout and creating a feature wall with a hand-printed wallpaper to lighten the interior, the space was transformed. We designed the restaurant around a window into the kitchen so guests could see the chefs in action and this has proved to be popular. We opted for the wine unit, tables and chairs to be in walnut and the chairs were covered in fabrics from the Scottish Island of Bute. Michaela found stylish tablemats, as we didn't want to have tablecloths (and still don't), and she even

Checking the bookings at The Kitchin.

sewed the curtains herself. Michaela has an eye for detail and added her special touch to the dining room and bar area to make a stylish but welcoming restaurant.

A month before we were set to open we met Philippe Nublat, who was to become our restaurant manager at The Kitchin. A charming Frenchman, Philippe was born in Marseille and spent more than 15 years working in top restaurants in France learning his trade before moving to Edinburgh to work and learn English. We liked him immediately and felt a connection so offered him the position of maître d', which he accepted. With Philippe on board, we spent the weeks leading up to the opening of the restaurant developing the wine list and bar list, employing staff, arranging various licenses for trading, and building up relationships with our suppliers while creating a menu fit for the Edinburgh market.

Sharing my world

My stag night – Raf, Jon, me, Gav, Chris and Massimo.

Pierre Koffmann once again came to my rescue when he told me that he was willing to sell me all his crockery, kitchen pots and pans, utensils, glassware and cutlery from the old La Tante Claire at a friendly price. I was completely taken aback. Michaela and I went down to his warehouse in Wimbledon to pick up the stuff and spent a week polishing, cleaning and sorting out plates, crockery, pots, pans, trays and glasses to get them ready for their re-launch.

As the wallpaper in the bar was still drying and we had our final checks and approvals on health and safety, fire alarms and licensing, to name but a few, we prepared for our opening night. The restaurant was starting to take shape. With the help of family and friends and our newly appointed PR company,

we sent out invitations for the opening night of The Kitchin. We invited 155 guests from the business, advertising and media sectors of Edinburgh and to our great surprise around 90 people showed up. I had to make my first-ever public speech and I was absolutely petrified but at the same time so incredibly excited and proud.

Still high on adrenalin, we had our first official day of trading on 1 June 2006 when we invited all the people and tradesman who had been involved with the creation of the restaurant. As I was looking out from the kitchen, through the window we had designed to be able to give diners a direct view into the kitchen, I was buzzing with excitement. I had three guys and a pot-washer with me in the kitchen and Philippe had one girl helping him on the restaurant floor. Michaela was meeting and greeting the guests and we had one girl in the bar. We had six staff employed and we were open – just about.

The Kitchin opened to the public on 3 June 2006, bang on target and within budget, thanks to strict adherence to our cash flow. We had two guests for lunch. My heart sank as I watched the restaurant through my kitchen window. I had asked my friend Raphael, my good friend and fellow-chef from my Koffmann years, to come up for that very first weekend and I felt that he was almost as excited about The Kitchin opening as I was. Thankfully, we had a few more guests for dinner, but for me it was one of the worst dinner services I have experienced to this day. I don't know if it was the pressure of finally being open, or the fact that none of us had ever worked together before, but nothing seemed to go right. Thank goodness Raphael was there to pick me up. In the days to follow, we discussed menus and ideas, and his calming influence made me feel slightly less anxious.

The first days of the new restaurant were some of the most daunting I have ever known and I felt more and more unsure about what the Scottish market was looking for. Were people expecting salmon and beef on the menu or should I cook the food that I liked eating? There were so many things to worry about. Needless to say, Michaela and I had some sleepless nights, as we worked through the figures, constantly updating the failing cash flow, redoing projections and thinking up new strategies.

On top of all that we decided to get married which turned out to be one of the best things we could have done. During June, in the first month of opening our restaurant, we were dealing with all the wedding arrangements as well as the many things to do with the restaurant. I recall walking home with Michaela

Our wedding day, 5 August 2006.

one night from the restaurant, when she started talking about table plans and who was sitting where. As much as I was looking forward to our marriage, I really could not switch my mind to wedding plans, I could think only of the next day – my menu and the food I wanted to cook, how to fill my empty restaurant and how we would survive.

I married my beautiful wife on 5 August 2006 and it was a truly spectacular day with family and friends from all over the world. A grand total of 20 countries were represented, which was quite a lot for a wedding of 100 guests. I had my stag night on the night before the wedding, on 4 August – just a few drinks in Leith with my closest mates. Having said that, I didn't actually have my first beer until just before midnight the day before the wedding, having served a restaurant full of family and friends that night. We spent a much-deserved wedding night at Prestonfield House in Edinburgh and decided to put our honeymoon on hold until our January break. We were both back at work the following day. Married and happy.

Business began to pick up as we entered autumn and I started to feel more adventurous about my menu. I could hear Koffmann's words in my head – cook what you want to cook! Cook from your heart! So I did. I changed the menu and started to experiment more with my dishes. I started to build up my relationship with my butcher, Peter Flockhart, and ask him for unusual products and cheaper, yet interesting and delicious cuts. I started to experiment with items such as pig's head, pig's ears, bone marrow and beef cheeks to mention just a few. Peter, like many of my suppliers, is now a frequent visitor to the restaurant as he enjoys tasting the dishes I have created with his outstanding produce. Some of the cheaper cuts of meat are only unpopular because they require greater knowledge and experience in preparation, but the flavour produces outstanding dishes. Having a one-to-one relationship with suppliers without the middleman is invaluable to me.

I introduced my new dishes on the set lunch menu to get feedback from diners and they soon turned out to be a hit. Then I put my pig's head dish on the à la carte menu and, as various papers and magazines reviewed us, food critics started referring to it as my signature dish. Top food critic Joanna Blythman was one of the first to taste my pig's head dish and gave us a great write-up. I was soon asked to do demonstrations around Scotland cooking pig's head and although the first one was nervewracking, I started to enjoy it because of the direct contact with the public.

My very first demonstration, and indeed my first public speaking appearance since my speech on the opening night at the restaurant, only happened because of Willie Pike at the Scottish Chefs' conference. Willie asked me to take part and had it not been for his great passion and commitment to young chefs, I am not sure I would have accepted. I was pretty scared as I went onto the stage that very first time, but I also believe that I offered something new and unusual to the Scottish audience – and, as I hoped, it attracted guests to the restaurant. To my amusement, my butcher called me one day and told me that all of a sudden customers were asking for pig's head. Although the dish takes me about 14 hours to prepare I started making a profit from it.

About four months after the opening of the restaurant, Pierre Koffmann asked to come up again. He was keen to see what we had been doing, having only had a glimpse of the restaurant on that crazy night before the wedding, and I was more than pleased to have the pleasure of his company. I think it gave him a thrill to see all his pots and pans, his old duck press, plates, glasses and cutlery being put to good use after a few years in a cold warehouse in Wimbledon.

As Koffmann put on his old Tante Claire chef's jacket and stood in the corner observing the stove, I felt an incredible shiver of excitement. The jacket was a bit tighter than it used to be, but Koffmann was still very much Chef and seeing him again brought back some strong memories. I had been slightly nervous about the thought of him coming up as I had no idea if he would leave me on my own or if he would start wanting to help me by pointing out things I was doing wrong. But all he did was observe. He didn't say much, just watched, and he insisted on trying everything that was cooked.

Pierre Koffmann visiting The Kitchin, October 2006.

A funny thing happened that night. Earlier in the day, I'd had a row with my kitchen porter and I had asked him to leave. The dishes were soon piling up and without batting an eyelid, Pierre Koffmann went straight to the kitchen porter's quarter, rolled up his sleeves and started helping out with the dirty dishes. My chefs didn't know what was happening. There was Koffmann, the mighty chef, tackling our pile of washing-up! To me, it was just another confirmation of his hands-on approach and I was not in the least surprised. We are chefs, not prima donnas, and I do believe that there should not be a single job in the kitchen that you won't do yourself. Nobody should feel above washing pots and pans and that is the way I run my kitchen.

Every night while Koffmann was there we sat down after service and he pointed out a few things which he liked, and suggested some improvements to my dishes. I was grateful that he waited until after service and didn't tell me anything in front of my guys. I listened and took every piece of advice on board.

In January 2007, my wife and I finally went on our belated honeymoon to St Lucia. It was our first chance to relax in over a year. But beautiful as the Caribbean was, I soon grew tired of the food, as most of the restaurants offered only pizza, pasta, hamburgers and chips. What I wanted was proper, home-made local cuisine. After a few days I came across a little hut at the end of the beach. I noticed a small boat going up to the hut a few times and I got curious. I went to investigate and found that the hut was a small but very primitive kitchen with a bar counter and a few chairs. The little boat was providing the woman in the shed with newly caught flying fish. I was over the moon with excitement, so ordered a beer and sat down to watch what she was doing. The woman's name was Marie and she was a local lady. This was her place and she was cooking lunch for the locals and tourists, if they could find her. Although the kitchen was incredibly primitive, with just about enough space for a cooker, a counter, a small sink and some shelves, she was preparing meals all made from local produce. There were flying fish, plantain and bananas, all with her own secret recipe, home-made sauces – and nutmegs for the spiced rum.

I didn't tell her I was a chef, but we started chatting about food and I asked if she could show me how to fillet flying fish, which she did. I went back to find Michaela and she couldn't believe it when she saw me stepping into Marie's kitchen, filleting flying fish and serving up dishes – while we were on our honeymoon! Luckily, she didn't mind.

Cooking with Marie while on honeymoon in St Lucia.

After that we had our lunch at Marie's most days and I spent a few hours working for Marie while the sun was at its peak. I loved it. The produce was fantastic – completely fresh and all local and I even picked up a few new techniques. Marie's food was absolutely outstanding and I was delighted to enjoy some good home-made Caribbean food at last.

The day after we came home, as we were preparing to re-open the restaurant, I received a phone call telling me The Kitchin had been awarded a Michelin star. I couldn't believe it! The star came only six months after opening and I was the youngest-ever chef proprietor in Scotland to receive one. Things changed overnight and bookings started rolling in.

A few days into being a Michelin-star restaurant, we hired a receptionist, Bridget. Under Michaela's guidance, she took over the front desk, as the phone had been ringing off the hook ever since the news had come out. Within the first week of the Michelin announcement, the telephone system had to be upgraded to cope with the high number of calls. The website also collapsed due to the sudden increase in number of hits and it dawned on us just how powerful the Michelin guide is and how many people swear by it. We recognised the need for a sommelier and we found one in Sylvain Ranc, a young, enthusiastic Frenchman with excellent wine knowledge.

For myself, Michaela, Philippe and the entire team at The Kitchin it was a lot to cope with. We didn't have enough staff, so we had to start recruiting. Unfortunately, the cash flow doesn't necessarily improve just because of a star but we didn't want to risk losing it. People said it was one of the fastest-achieved stars and I didn't want to become known as the fastest to lose it as well! They were frightening days, but although riding high on the Michelin buzz I continued to push my suppliers and it soon paid off.

Sharing my world

I remember calling my game supplier one day, pressing for the last woodcock around and he managed to get his hands on a few. As a restaurateur you never know who will walk through the door, and sure enough the respected food critic Terry Durack came to the restaurant that night and sampled the very last woodcock of the season. As a result, he listed his meal at The Kitchin as one of his most memorable of the year in his column in *The Independent*. This was a great achievement for us and certainly attracted a few new diners to the restaurant.

Following the news of the star came far more media interest than we had ever anticipated and Michaela and I took every chance to meet journalists and increase our public profile. But with the star and media exposure came greater pressure and expectations from diners. As much as we were delighted with the achievement, our greatest concerns were to achieve a healthy cash flow and see many satisfied customers. The obvious thing was to re-invest every penny into the business and try to improve the facilities, which we had not been able to do initially as we were on such a tight budget. One of the first investments we made was to build another wine unit, which could hold 150 bottles. We also built shelves and storage units in the bar to make operations smoother. When we closed for our first summer break, we made alterations to the kitchen and the following summer we installed air conditioning. These changes were all necessary and in line with the natural progression of our rapidly developing business.

Philippe spent a lot of time developing and improving the wine list. With the newly increased storage space, we were able to expand the list and add some fantastic new and unusual wines to our collection. When we first opened The Kitchin we had a wine list of 30 bins and six staff. Two years later we were reaching 220 bins and 23 staff. This was a necessary progression in order to keep our high standards but a frightening one at the same time, due to the high costs involved.

Although we were pretty desperate to hire staff after the Michelin announcement, we remained determined to find the right people – people who shared our passion and saw hospitality as a career and not just a way of earning a bit of extra money at the weekend. A friend put me in touch with David Williams, who turned out to be the only one of my kitchen brigade who was with me from the start and stayed for more than a year. After six months Ron McKinlay from Canada joined us and to this day I am grateful to both him and David for sticking it out, as I was going through periods of losing and replacing two chefs a week at times.

Many young chefs were naturally curious about what we were doing in The Kitchin and approached me for work. I would always offer anyone who I felt had potential a day's work experience to see how they got on, as it also gave them a chance to see how they felt about working with me. Many young boys and girls who told me they had worked as sous-chefs and even as head chefs did not know the basics of cooking or had completely the wrong attitude to work and were not suited to my kitchen. I can't stand a loudmouth, especially if it's someone who has nothing to be loud about. You must learn how to walk before you run. However, I must admit that on a few occasions I began to wonder if I was demanding too much from my chefs, but I was convinced that there were young chefs out there with the same passion as mine. The only thing I know is hard work and in my eyes you don't succeed unless you push yourself to your limits and work for it. The Kitchin was becoming a hard school for young chefs but I couldn't imagine having it any other way.

At one point there were only three of us in the kitchen, plus Alamin, our Sudanese kitchen porter, and we were all doing everything, working flat out. I was back working shifts of 17 or 18 hours again. I was determined to achieve my dream of a successful restaurant and it gave me an incredible thrill to be surrounded by people who wanted to work with me towards this goal. On a few occasions I brought my best friend Oliver into the kitchen to help out. Ollie was chopping vegetables, making canapés and serving up the amuse-bouche and I loved having him around. Alamin was trained to identify the different meat and fish and take them out of the fridges during service to help speed things up. As the orders came in, he provided the different produce for the chefs to cook. I was always confident that I would get more staff willing to go through the same hard school I did as a young chef in training. It was just a matter of finding them.

Soon afterwards, we employed Roberta, an Edinburgh-born girl Michaela had worked with in Dubai. Everybody in my kitchen is treated the same and Roberta has been holding her own in our male-dominated kitchen and is still with me to this day. I was now slowly building my team around me and we were all working hard and very long hours.

In the following months we received more awards and recognition than I had ever anticipated in my wildest dreams. I was incredibly proud but it just made me want to put my head down and work even harder. I have never cooked for accolades and awards and never will. I just want to cook food that I enjoy eating. I appreciate how much accolades can do for your business in terms of awareness and getting guests through the door, and I am grateful for the recognition we have received, but to me cooking has always been more about achieving personal satisfaction than anything else. Any accolade is a bonus but the most important thing is to be happy with the food you create.

Although there were more of us at this point than when we started, my kitchen brigade was too small to create the more ambitious dishes I wanted to cook and we certainly couldn't afford any more wage bills. However, as we got more established, I slowly started to push my limits and those of my chefs. By incorporating many techniques and ideas I had picked up from working with the great chefs, I wanted to take my own philosophy and ideas to the next level and allow myself to be more adventurous.

When I was asked to do the Great British Menu on BBC in the autumn of 2007, I had many reservations but one of the greatest was that of leaving my kitchen. Although we had managed to arrange most of the filming on my days off, it also involved a few, unavoidable, days away. Had I been asked a year earlier I would have said no, but considering how beneficial this could be for the business, I accepted, and Pierre Koffmann offered to come up and run the kitchen for a week. I didn't tell the competition judges about this arrangement, but one of them, Prue Leith,

The Kitchin team.

Sharing my world

Two-week-old Kasper with Pierre Koffmann.

Kasper Kitchin arrived on 21 February 2008 and at 10 pounds he certainly made a grand entrance into this world. To have Kasper in our lives is definitely the most beautiful thing anyone could ask for and we both settled to parenthood more easily than I had ever imagined. There is no denying that having a baby and running your own busy restaurant can be tricky at times, but we have managed to make sure Kasper is our priority at all times, while still managing to get on with our lives.

Michaela was back at work within a matter of days, often with Kasper on one arm. My wife finds it as hard as I do to let go, and when it's your own business you simply make it work. Kasper was with her everywhere she went in the first few months and she managed to work around him. Nowadays we have other arrangements in place which allow Michaela to combine motherhood with her vital full-time role in the business. Kasper loves the staff and they have been brilliant and patient with him. I believe Kasper has brought our whole team closer together. I always make a point of spending an hour or two with Kasper and Michaela during my afternoon break, as that is our proper family time. I know that this is more than many people who are tied to office hours get to see their kids and I treasure every minute with my son. Now that Kasper has discovered his liking for food, we always cook for him – and of course I always use seasonal ingredients! How could I not when I'm so passionate about good food, and Kasper enjoys it!

told me one day that some of her friends had been to The Kitchin and thought they had seen Pierre Koffmann behind the stove. They couldn't believe their eyes. I told her it was true – my mentor and friend had come to my rescue.

In the early days, with such a small team I got obsessed with doing everything myself, not letting anyone else take on my responsibilities as I was so afraid of losing everything I had worked so hard for. Thankfully, I have since learnt to delegate, but I still speak to my suppliers daily and always make a point of speaking with many of our guests after their meal. I have never been a big-headed person, but I always believed in our restaurant and I believed in my food. My confidence grew with the feedback from the diners, but I am still to this day adamant that I don't leave my kitchen unless it's an absolute necessity and to the advantage of the business – with the exception of when my son was born.

In March 2008 I was asked to go to New York to represent Scotland for The Tartan Week, renamed *Scotland Week*. My wife and five-week old son were able to join me for a week of promotional chats, cooking demonstrations, and television and radio interviews. It was a busy week, but fantastic exposure for Scotland in the US.

With the economic downturn in autumn 2008, we entered a new phase in the business. The changes in the exchange rate with the euro affected our wine prices and increased our supplier costs, which made us very cautious of the changing market. Although we noticed fluctuations in the lunch trade we took several steps to make sure that our cash flow remained strong. We spent most mornings going over projections, which changed daily, and we examined the ever-changing market to make sure we kept a financial cushion in place so we remain in full control of the business.

By constantly discussing strategies and maintaining and improving standards to ensure customer satisfaction I keep a close eye on my margins and constantly talk to the suppliers about keener deals and maintaining quality. Although I've no accountancy skills, I have learnt to see the consequences of how a small percentage change in the strength of the pound can suddenly turn a profit into a loss. I know exactly what is happening every day in my business but I'm the first to admit that sometimes I wish I had more time to reflect on the business while still remaining creative and on top of my game.

Thankfully, The Kitchin now has a great team, with each member strong in his or her own department, and I rely heavily on my wife, my dad and Philippe as well as the other people around me to be as efficient as possible. In January 2009, we introduced 'Your Kitchin', a new service created in response to customer demand to give guests the opportunity of enjoying fine dining at their home or office. We also developed our own range of fine chocolates, thanks to my pastry chef Sebastian, who was a runner-up in the World Chocolate Master final. Seb makes truly outstanding chocolates so this was a natural step for us and one that generates additional revenue.

I believe people will always seek out top-quality food that is good value for money and I am convinced that diners will continue coming to The Kitchin if we constantly improve our services and food standards. I strive to develop new ideas and recipes by reading cookbooks and speaking to fellow chefs, and I appreciate that knowing different techniques and butchery skills are vital in order to experiment with different produce. I often have young people coming to my kitchen for work experience and I encourage this, as it is a great way of training.

Over the last few months I have had the great pleasure of sharing my kitchen with my old friend and fellow chef Dominic Jack. Since leaving the Gleneagles Hotel all these years ago, he has followed a similar career path to my own, going through the equally hard kitchens of Michel Perraud at Fleur de Sel in England, and Alain Passard at L'Arpège, Alain Solivérès at Hotel Vernet and Taillevent, all in Paris, as well as being chef de cuisine at the prestigious Swissotel in Istanbul. I love working with Dominic again and exchanging ideas and ways of improving and creating new dishes. I admire his fantastic cooking skills and I look forward to creating a strong business relationship once the economic climate has improved.

I was once again able to do some filming for the BBC's Great British Menu in 2009 as well as appearing on a few other cooking shows, thanks to the support of Dominic and the team. I still only ever leave my kitchen when it's absolutely essential, as I want to encourage customers through the door and spread the word about The Kitchin. By ensuring consistency at all times and never allowing my high standards to slip I aim to develop the business further and continue my exciting seasonal journey – From Nature to Plate.

Spring

Spring is the proper beginning of my kitchen year and a season that I look forward to with great anticipation. By the time spring arrives I am desperate to welcome all the spring produce into my kitchen and I long to work with fresh green vegetables again. As much as I love root vegetables, such as celeriac and parsnips, and the heavier meat and game dishes, I'm ready to leave those behind with winter and begin a new adventure.

Somehow spring always gives me a little bit of a bounce in my feet – I feel like I want to kick off my shoes and dance around in my kitchen. Not that I do, of course, but I feel lighter somehow. My adrenalin kicks in with spring and so does the level of excitement, as I think about all the produce that is about to come in.

The moment spring arrives I'm eager to cook peas, broad beans, green asparagus and other fresh vegetables! I want to create lighter, brighter dishes and I can't wait to get my hands on the first greens and the first morels, not to mention the first wild Scottish salmon. Thanks to my network of trusted suppliers, I always get the first produce of the season delivered to my restaurant as soon as it is possible. I want my customers to experience and understand the beauty of locally grown produce and to try things the minute they are available so they can taste how incredibly fresh the ingredients really are. I also want them to understand the relationship between seasonality and flavours. One of the most important things to remember is to allow the seasons to inspire your dishes and help you make natural matches. Wild spring herbs, such as sorrel, sweet cicely and wild garlic, as well as spring salad leaves and green lettuce served with wild salmon, wild sea trout, lamb or rabbit are marriages made in heaven.

Throughout the entire spring season, I am on the phone to my suppliers, asking when I can have things, how much they are, how good? To any chef or cook, price and quality are incredibly important. I always want to be certain that the quality of

Spring

my produce is the best I can get and I am not overcharged. As a chef, I know you need to pay top dollar at the start of the season – and you're prepared to do it to get the right produce. However, as the season goes on and more produce becomes available, the price should go down and good seasonal produce should be available to everyone.

I like to have a close relationship with my suppliers and I always make a point of knowing exactly where my produce is from, and finding out the name of the farmer, fisherman or diver if I can. I share this information with my diners by putting the origin of my produce on the menu. I mention where the produce is from, who has grown or caught it and how – for example, for a scallop dish I always add that that the scallops are hand-dived by Robert, my supplier. I believe this information helps people to understand my passion for quality produce. Over the years, the

suppliers have become a vital part of my business and I only ever use suppliers who are as passionate about their produce as I am about my cooking. I feel strongly that their names should be mentioned on my menu, as they deserve it.

Soon after we opened the restaurant, a young man showed up at the back door one morning, saying he was a forager. He had a list of everything he had foraged the day before and asked if I was interested. There was wood sorrel, wild rocket flowers, wild mint and other wild herbs from the local woods and riverbanks. I was pretty impressed with his knowledge. The lad's name was Ben and he was 21 and still at university, but he wanted to develop the skills he had picked up from his father about nature and wildlife and make a few pennies. After graduation, he set up his own business – Fungi and Forage. He spends two days foraging in the woods

and riverbanks, followed by one day trading, and he delivers the very freshest, newly picked produce to my kitchen. I have no idea how many young foragers there are out there, but I support them and they certainly make an impression on me with their dedication and knowledge of nature.

I can admit to being almost fanatical about the seasons, but spring is always that bit special, simply because it symbolises many things other than cooking. Not only do you turn the clock forwards and get that important extra hour of daylight, which makes a massive difference in the early hours of the day, but it is also the beginning of a new chapter. A chef who doesn't understand seasonality and who doesn't want to work in tune with the seasons still has a long way to go in my eyes. Cooking is all about using the produce available around you, minimising

food miles and supporting your local farmers. Whatever you can get from the land and sea on your doorstep will always be superior to food that is not in season. It is indeed tempting for any professional chef to cook in order to win accolades, but although they mean a lot and can have a tremendous impact on your business, the most important thing is to cook for your own palate and cook from the heart. Same goes for the home cook: cooking with seasonal vegetables, meat and fish will always give the best results.

For me, many menus in this country are unbalanced and uninteresting, and it is often down to the simple fact that the chef does not work in tune with the seasons. As most produce is available all year around, seasonality seems to be forgotten. When I see dishes with strawberries or asparagus

served in the middle of winter in Scotland I know they are most definitely not local. The flavours are just not the same as they are in spring and summer and you can never achieve a good result with these out-of-season ingredients.

Scottish peas are definitely a favourite of mine – simply delicious! I remember eating peas in the fields behind our house in Pittendreich when I was younger because I loved their sweet taste. Years later when working on the Bamfords' yacht, passionately exploring the many food markets of southern Europe every morning, it was again brought home to me just how delicious fresh peas really are. The taste of peas symbolises spring and I believe the delicious green flavour brightens up the plate. At the restaurant, I do get my very first peas directly from the South of France as they come into season much earlier than those in Scotland. The same goes for other green spring vegetables, but their taste cannot be faulted and it certainly triggers my excitement about what is soon to come from Scottish farms.

One of the great events in spring is the arrival of the first wild Scottish salmon. I remember being on the phone to Willie Little, one of my suppliers, after receiving the first salmon of the year, and claiming that they were almost too small to use at the restaurant. Willie replied without hesitation, 'Tom, you won't get any big ones until the rain comes.'

The younger, smaller salmon (grilse) are the ones which can swim up the rivers first and the larger salmon must wait until there is enough water in the rivers. The extraordinary story of the salmon's life – the fact that it makes its way from the river of its birth, out into the Atlantic, and then back to the exact spot in the river where it hatched – has always fascinated me and is one of Nature's great wonders. The thought that all this happens before it shows up in the fish van at my restaurant brings a smile to my face.

Another highlight at this time of year is the birth of the spring lamb, although in Scotland you're not allowed to eat them as early as you are in France. Rump of lamb is my absolute favourite, although I also love Barnsley chops, especially when served with kidneys and sweetbreads. The reason why lamb goes so well with peas is because they are perfectly in tune, both spring foods. Both are at their prime at the same time and this is a natural but obvious match of gorgeous flavours that complement each other fully in cooking.

The menu at The Kitchin changes entirely with the seasons but I also add dishes at any time if I get my hands on special produce. I like to have the flexibility to play with new ideas and give our diners more choices. I always push myself and the team that little bit extra in springtime, as I know the energy is there and the possibilities are that much greater than in the darker months of the year. Spring is an outstanding period in the kitchen.

Leek and potato soup
with crispy ox tongue and poached egg

Serves 4

Here, I have taken a traditional soup recipe and added my own modern touch to it. The ox tongue and the poached egg make the soup much more interesting.

2 white onions, peeled and finely sliced	**Ox tongue**	**Eggs**
150g unsalted butter	1 large onion	4 free-range eggs
4 leeks (green tops), washed and finely sliced	1 large carrot	100ml white wine vinegar
3 medium potatoes, peeled and finely sliced	4 celery sticks	salt
	2 leeks	
	1 bunch of parsley stalks	**Garnish**
	1 head of garlic, broken into cloves	100g leeks (white parts), washed and finely sliced
	1 bouquet garni (see p.265)	knob of butter
	1 fresh ox tongue, about 2kg	100g potato, peeled and cut into 2cm cubes
	1 teaspoon vegetable oil	

To serve
Put some leek and potato garnish in the centre of each soup bowl and place an egg on top. Pour the soup around and serve with crispy ox tongue.

To make the soup
- In a heavy-bottomed pan, sweat the sliced onions gently in the butter for 4–5 minutes. Add the sliced leeks and sweat for another 2 minutes. Add the potatoes, cover with about 1 litre of boiling water and boil over a high heat until the potatoes are cooked.

- Remove from the heat and blitz the soup in a blender until smooth. Do this as quickly as possible to keep the lovely green colour.

To cook the ox tongue
- Bring a large pot of seasoned water to the boil. Dice all the vegetables, add them to the pan with garlic and bouquet garni, and bring back to the boil. Then add the tongue and reduce the heat to a simmer. Cook for about 4 hours or until the meat is very tender.

- Once the tongue is cooked, lift it out and carefully remove the skin while it is still warm. Also remove any glands, excess fat and gristle, then leave the tongue to rest and set in the fridge for at least 30 minutes. Cut it into cubes and then fry in a heated, oiled pan until golden brown and crispy on both sides.

To poach the eggs
- Bring a pan of water to the boil and add the vinegar and a pinch of salt. Gently whisk the water to create a whirlpool effect, then drop in the eggs and cook for 3–4 minutes for soft yolks. Remove the eggs and place them on kitchen paper to drain.

To prepare the garnish
- Gently sweat the leeks in a pan with a knob of butter and season with salt and pepper. Boil the potatoes for 4–5 minutes until soft.

If you can't get ox tongue, bacon works just as well.
Just dice and fry until crispy.

Baby artichokes
with peppers, pesto and Parmesan

If you can't get fresh baby artichokes, good delis usually store excellent marinated ones, which work just as well in this recipe.

6 baby artichokes
1 lemon
2 tablespoons diced onion
1 carrot, peeled and diced
1 rasher bacon, diced
1 teaspoon olive oil
150ml white wine
1 litre chicken stock (see p.258)

Pesto
2 garlic cloves
2 teaspoons pine nuts
150ml olive oil
100g fresh basil leaves
25g Parmesan cheese, grated

Peppers and garnish
4 red peppers
olive oil
25g black olives
30g Parmesan cheese

To serve
Place some red pepper in the middle of each plate. Put 2 halves of artichoke on top and drizzle pesto on and around. Add olives and thin shavings of Parmesan.

To prepare the artichokes
* Peel away the tough outer leaves of the artichokes. Trim the tops of the soft green leaves, cut the artichokes in half and remove the furry cores with a melon baller. Rub with a cut lemon to stop the artichokes turning brown.

* Sauté the diced onion, carrot and bacon in the olive oil. Add the peeled and halved artichokes and deglaze the pan with white wine. Cook until the wine is reduced by half and then cover with two-thirds of the chicken stock. Put a lid on the pan and cook the artichokes as quickly as possible until they are tender, adding more chicken stock as required. Strain the mixture through a sieve, then take out the artichokes and put them in the stock until needed. Discard all the other vegetables and the bacon.

To make the pesto
* In a blender or food processor, blitz the garlic and pine nuts with one spoonful of olive oil. Add the basil and Parmesan, then slowly pour in the rest of olive oil until well mixed.

To prepare the peppers and garnish
* Preheat the oven to 170°C/Gas 3. Place the red peppers on an oven tray and pour a little olive oil over them. Cover the peppers with aluminium foil and roast for 20 minutes, turning after 10 minutes. Leave to cool, then remove skin and seeds and cut into thin strips. Season with salt. Halve or slice the olives as desired. Slice shavings of Parmesan with a vegetable peeler.

Spring vegetable crudités
with tapenade and pesto

Serves 4

I've always enjoyed eating crudités in the South of France, and I was inspired to do a Scottish version with wonderful fresh spring vegetables.

6 young carrots	**Tapenade**	**Pesto (see opposite)**
1 cucumber	200g black olives, pitted	
12 young radishes	50g tinned anchovy fillets	
2 fennel bulbs	50g capers	
6 asparagus spears	2 tablespoons olive oil	
15 pods of broad beans	salt and pepper	

To prepare the vegetables

- Peel the carrots and cut them into finger-length strips. Cut the cucumber into similar-sized strips. Cut the radishes in half. Cut the fennel in half and then slice each half into 4 neat wedges. Trim the asparagus and peel the stalks, and pod the broad beans. Cover all vegetables with a wet kitchen cloth or wet kitchen paper until just about to serve, as this will keep them fresh and moist.

To make the tapenade

- Place all the ingredients in a blender and blitz until smooth. Season with salt and pepper to taste and keep in the fridge until ready to use.

- Make the pesto as for the recipe opposite.

To serve

Arrange all the vegetables neatly together on a large serving plate or tray and serve with separate bowls of tapenade and pesto on the side for everyone to help themselves.

Adding an ice cube or two to the mixture when making the pesto helps keep the pesto an intense green.

Eggs en cocotte

This is a great Sunday supper. I sometimes add smoked haddock or smoked salmon instead of bacon.

100g button mushrooms	Mornay sauce
100g bacon rashers	60g butter
100g broad beans	60g plain flour
250g fresh spinach	1 litre milk
2 teaspoons olive oil	4 gratings of nutmeg
salt	salt and pepper
4 free-range eggs	100g Mull Cheddar, grated

To serve

Serve straight from the oven. The dishes will be piping hot, so place them on a plate.

To make the mornay sauce

- In a medium saucepan, melt the butter and add the flour. Whisk over a low heat for 2–3 minutes until there are no lumps. Bring the milk to the boil with a little grated nutmeg and pour it over the cooked roux. Bring to the boil and cook for 10 minutes, stirring gently. Season, pass through a sieve and stir in the grated cheese.

To prepare the vegetables and bacon

- Wipe the mushrooms and cut them into quarters. Cut the bacon into 1cm batons and sauté together with mushrooms for 3 or 4 minutes. Pod the broad beans and blanch them for 1 minute in boiling salted water. Refresh them in a bowl of iced water and then peel off the tough outer skins. Wash the spinach and dry on some paper towels. Heat the olive oil in a medium pan, add the spinach and a pinch of salt, and cook until the spinach is wilted.

Assembling the dish

- Preheat the oven to 180°C/Gas 4. You will need four ovenproof dishes. Place some spinach in each dish and cover with mornay sauce. Crack an egg on top, sprinkle with broad beans and bacon, and season with salt and pepper. Put the dishes in a baking tin, pour in boiling water to come half way up the sides of the dishes and bake for 8–10 minutes. The egg yolks should still be soft.

Pea soup
with crab

This pea soup is simplicity itself to prepare, but the crab garnish makes it into a really special dish.

400g fresh peas (podded weight)
30g butter
salt and pepper

Crab garnish
½ red pepper
50g peas (podded weight)
20 black olives
handful of fresh basil
160g white crabmeat

1 lime
1 lemon
200ml crème fraîche
small bunch of chives, chopped

To make the soup
- Bring a litre of water to the boil, add salt and the peas, and cook for 3–4 minutes or until soft. Blend with some of the cooking water and the butter until you have the consistency you want, then pass through a sieve. Cool over a bowl of ice water so the soup keeps its lovely green colour.

To prepare the crab garnish
- Peel the red pepper with a vegetable peeler, remove the seeds and dice finely. Blanch the peas in boiling water for 15 seconds. Chop the black olives and cut the basil into strips.

- Mix the pepper, peas, olives and basil with the crab and season with salt and pepper. Zest the lime and lemon. Whisk the crème fraîche with the juice of half the lime until it forms soft peaks, then add the zest and chopped chives.

To serve
Place some of the crab mixture in a ring in the centre of each bowl. Pour some pea soup around the crab and add a small scoop of crème fraîche on top of the crab.

Asparagus

The Scottish asparagus season starts at the beginning of May and goes on until the middle of June. The season is short, only six weeks, but the quality of the asparagus is exceptional. English asparagus is available shortly before the Scottish and the French even earlier than that, and although I am devoted to seasonal produce, I don't mind using English or French asparagus to stretch the brief season a little further.

Before I went away to work in France for 12 years I have to admit I couldn't quite understand all the fuss about asparagus. I saw it on menus all year round in Scotland and often found it bland. But while working in France I discovered how truly beautiful asparagus is and how much fun it is to cook – not to mention its incredible flavour. It was only when I returned to Scotland to set up the restaurant that I realised the excellence of Scottish asparagus – it is definitely as good as anything you can get elsewhere in Europe, if not better.

Unfortunately, although asparagus is so common on menus in this country, many people are disappointed by it, usually because it is served out of season and has been flown in from thousands of miles away. As asparagus is easy to cook and looks great on the plate, some chefs don't pay proper attention to the flavours and don't seem to care that fresh locally sourced asparagus is as different from out-of-season produce as night and day. I firmly believe that anyone who has eaten completely fresh, local asparagus, cooked to perfection, will always remember the flavour, as it is so unique and delicious.

Because the asparagus season is short, I treasure every spear I manage to get my hands on. As soon as a box of newly picked asparagus arrives at the restaurant, I soak the spears in ice-cold water for 10–15 minutes so they keep their intense green colour. I lay them out on a tray, making sure that no tips are damaged, and place a wet cloth on top to keep them moist until I'm ready to cook. Then I remove all the little points on the stems and cut the spears to the size I want. All the trimmings, except the woody hard bits at the bottom, I chop up and use in a sauce or to make an amuse-bouche at the restaurant.

When I spent a day at my supplier's asparagus farm recently he gave me one or two spears directly from the ground to eat. The flavour was intense and

juicy and the texture had that little bit of crunchiness you only get in raw vegetables that are really fresh. I buy my asparagus from Sandy Pattullo of Eassie Farm near Glamis Castle, about an hour from Edinburgh. The Pattullos have a small family-run business and their produce is outstanding, a true confirmation of Scotland's fantastic produce. The soil of this region is very fertile and, thanks to a good drainage system that enables the soil to dry quickly, it is ideal for asparagus. I was surprised when my supplier told me that heavy frosts in winter don't affect the asparagus crops much, but heavy rain can do enormous damage and that is why good drainage

is so important. If the asparagus plants are lying in water, the quality is seriously affected and the crop can even be destroyed.

Although the asparagus-growing season is short, the preparations can sometimes take years to perfect. Planting starts at the beginning of April when the weather is warming up, but the asparagus are not usually ready to crop for another two years, or sometimes even longer. The Scottish asparagus grow more slowly than the French ones, and it has been suggested that this has an effect on the colour of the vegetable – the Scottish asparagus being slightly lighter in colour than its British counterpart. In

the right conditions, an asparagus grower might get up to 15 spears from one plant in the short growing season. The asparagus grow fast if the weather is good, meaning they can shoot up as much as 7.5cm a day in a warm spell. I remember speaking to Sandy Pattullo on a sunny day in the middle of the asparagus season when the temperature was reaching 20°C. He said, 'When I was picking today, I could almost sense the asparagus growing behind me in the field'. I loved that. Legend has it that if you lie down in an asparagus field all day, you can watch the asparagus grow with your own eyes, but I've never had the time to try this for myself!

restaurants like mine. The men and women who pick the asparagus in the fields carefully check each and every one with a measuring stick to ensure perfection. Those asparagus that are de-formed or thinner or shorter than the standard size are termed kitchen-asparagus, or soup asparagus, and sold to restaurants and suppliers for a cheaper price. The flavour is still the same but the physical attributes are not up to standard. Asparagus spears are usually cut when 22–25cm long. Although the picking process is done by hand, machinery can now help with some of the grading and separation of the asparagus once picked. This obviously speeds up the procedure but

During the few weeks of the growing season, Sandy and his wife gather their friends and neighbours from the surrounding area to help with the asparagus. If the weather is hot, they need more people than during the colder days, simply because there are more asparagus to handle. Everyone is involved in the different parts of the process; from the harvesting to bunching up the spears and loading the bunches into boxes ready to sell or send off to

it also means less contact with humans – it seems that the quality of asparagus is better when fewer people touch the produce.

Asparagus is one of those vegetables you don't need to do a lot with to make a delicious dish and I always like to serve it as simply as possible. My favourite recipes include asparagus served with hollandaise sauce, or roasted asparagus served with langoustines or poached eggs.

Asparagus hollandaise

This traditional dish makes an ideal starter for a spring dinner party. The hollandaise can be made in advance, so all that needs to be done when the guests arrive is to cook the asparagus and spoon over the sauce.

20 large asparagus spears	**Hollandaise sauce**
salt	4 egg yolks
400ml balsamic vinegar	250g clarified butter
	(see p.264)
	juice of ½ lemon
	salt

To serve

Place some asparagus on each plate. Pour the hollandaise over the stems and drizzle with the reduced balsamic.

To prepare the asparagus

- Remove the little points from the asparagus stems with a sharp knife and trim off the woody bases. Tie the asparagus spears in a bundle with string so they are all facing the same way.

- Take a large pan and add about 2 litres of water and a good handful of salt. Taste the water to make sure it is quite salty. Bring the water to boil, then plunge the asparagus into the pan and cook for 6–7 minutes until tender. Check that the asparagus are cooked by gently piercing a stem with a knife. If the knife enters gently, the asparagus is cooked; if there is still resistance, leave the asparagus in the water for another minute. Remove the asparagus, take off the string and put the spears on a plate.

To prepare the balsamic vinegar

- Pour the balsamic vinegar into a saucepan and reduce over a medium heat until the texture becomes syrup-like and coats the back of a spoon.

To prepare the hollandaise sauce

- Bring a saucepan of water to the boil. Put the egg yolks into a bowl that fits over the saucepan and add two tablespoons of water. Place the mixing bowl over the pan of simmering water and whisk until the egg yolks foam and then thicken. Reduce the heat and cook the yolks until they have the consistency of cream. Using a spatula, keep scraping the sides of a bowl to keep the eggs from scrambling. When you can see the bottom of the bowl as you whisk, it is time to stop cooking.

- Remove the bowl from the heat and whisk until the eggs have cooled and you are able to hold your hand against the bowl without discomfort. Put the bowl on top of a folded tea towel to keep it steady. Season to taste, then pour a thin stream of clarified butter into the bowl, whisking constantly until all the butter has been incorporated. Add the lemon juice, season and the sauce is ready to serve.

Once the hollandaise is cooked, keep it in a warm place so that the sauce doesn't split.

Asparagus, smoked bacon and langoustines

Serves 4

Langoustines are naturally meaty and their flavour makes a great match with the asparagus and the smoky bacon. I like to cook the langoustines whole so everyone can can get stuck in and enjoy peeling the shellfish themselves.

40g smoked bacon
16 asparagus spears
2 teaspoons olive oil
8 large live langoustines
salt and pepper

To prepare the bacon and asparagus

- Cut the bacon into strips 5cm long and 0.5cm wide, put them in a small pan and cover with cold water. Place the pan over a high heat until the water is just about to boil. Remove the bacon strips and plunge them into a bowl of ice water. Cool, strain and set aside.

- Peel and trim the asparagus stems. Warm a teaspoon of olive oil in a large heavy-bottomed pan over medium heat and roast the asparagus spears. Move them around every minute or so to prevent them burning. After 5 minutes, add the bacon and cook until bacon is crispy and the asparagus is done.

To prepare the langoustines

- Heat another pan and add 1 teaspoon of olive oil. Add the langoustines and cook for about 6 minutes, turning them halfway through. Season with some salt and pepper.

To serve

Arrange the asparagus and bacon on a plate and place the langoustines alongside.

Always ask for local asparagus rather than imported
– the flavour will be far superior.

Smoked mackerel
with sweet potato and watercress

If you don't want to smoke the mackerel yourself, buy smoked mackerel from the supermarket or your fishmonger. It will work just as well.

2 x 300g fresh mackerel	Sweet potato	Watercress purée
juice of 1 lemon	400g sweet potato	100g watercress
olive oil	20g butter	100ml double cream
salt	salt and pepper	salt and pepper

Garnish
1 sweet potato
100ml vegetable oil

To serve
Spoon a circle of watercress purée onto each plate and place some cubes of sweet potato inside the circle. Place a fillet of smoked mackerel on top and garnish with the crispy sweet potatoes.

To smoke the mackerel
- Fillet the mackerel. Brush the fillets with lemon juice, olive oil and salt and leave them aside for 10 minutes at room temperature. Gently wash the fillets in cold water to remove any excess salt and pat dry with a paper towel. Smoke in a smoking machine for 8–10 minutes. Remove from the smoker, place the fish on a plate and carefully remove all the pin bones with tweezers.

To prepare the sweet potato
- Peel the sweet potato and cut into dice measuring about 2cm. Put the dice in a large heavy-bottomed frying pan, add water to cover and place over medium heat. Add the butter, season with salt and pepper and cook until the potato is softened. Drain and set aside.

To prepare the watercress purée
- Bring a large pot of water to a rapid boil, season and add the watercress. Cook for 2 minutes, then remove and immediately place in a bowl of ice water – this helps retain the green colour. Drain in a fine sieve, squeezing out all the excess water. In a clean pan, heat the double cream to a gentle simmer and add the strained watercress. Season to taste and then blend to a smooth purée. Leave to chill in the fridge until ready to use.

To prepare the garnish
- Peel the sweet potato, slice very thinly and cut into thin strips. Fry the strips in vegetable oil until crispy, then drain on kitchen paper and season.

Mackerel is a cheap, under-rated fish but incredibly good for you, and also one of the very best fish to smoke.

Sea bass en papillote
with carrot, leek and ginger

Make sure everyone is seated at the table when you take the papillotes out of the oven. They will only stay puffed up for about a minute before they deflate, so bring them to the table for everyone to see and serve straight away.

2 x 200g sea bass fillets	2 teaspoons olive oil	2 spring onions, chopped
1 carrot	½ fennel bulb	salt and pepper
½ leek	500ml fish stock	
20g root ginger	zest of ½ lemon	

To prepare the fish and vegetables
- Remove the skin from the sea bass fillets. Peel the carrot and cut into julienne strips. Remove the outer layers of the leek and cut into fine strips. Peel the ginger (keep the skin for the stock) and cut into fine strips. Sauté the ginger in a teaspoon of olive oil, add the carrots and leek and cook for 3–4 minutes. Season to taste and set aside.

To make the fennel stock
- Heat 1 teaspoon of olive oil in a saucepan. Chop the fennel finely and sauté together with the skin of the ginger. Pour in the fish stock to cover the fennel and cook for 15 minutes. Remove the pan from the heat and set aside so the stock can infuse for 20 minutes. Pass it through a fine sieve, keeping the liquid but discarding the vegetables.

To make the papillotes
- Preheat the oven to 180°C/Gas 4. Cut a circle of greaseproof paper measuring about 20cm in diameter and place it on a A3-sized piece of aluminium foil. Place half the leek and ginger mixture in the centre of the greaseproof circle. Add a sea bass fillet and top with some lemon zest, spring onion, salt and pepper. Pour 100ml of the fennel fish stock onto the sea bass. Place another sheet of foil on top of the sea bass and fold in the edges to make a tightly sealed parcel. Make the other parcel in the same way. If making this dish for four people, put two pieces of fish in each parcel.

- Put the papillotes on an ovenproof pan and heat the pan on top of the stove until the parcels start to expand. Cook in the preheated oven for 5 minutes.

To serve
At the table, open the papillotes with a sharp knife and use a spatula to serve the fish and vegetables onto warm plates. Pour over the juices.

Oyster jelly
with broccoli and smoked salmon

Serves 4

If you eat oysters often, I think it is well worth investing in a good oyster knife. This makes opening the oysters much easier and protects you from injury.

½ leaf gelatin
4 oysters
2 limes
1 small head of broccoli
20g smoked salmon

- Soak the gelatin in enough water to cover. Open the oysters and strain the oyster juice through a fine sieve. Clean the oysters and the shells by rinsing them in cold water. Set the oysters aside.

To serve
Serve the oysters on a bed of sea salt with a wedge of fresh lime.

- Heat the oyster juice gently with a squeeze of lime juice. Make sure it doesn't boil. Squeeze out the soaked gelatin and add it to the juice to make a jelly.

- Trim the broccoli into tiny florets and blanch them in boiling water. Cut the smoked salmon into small triangles.

- Place each oyster back into its shell and cover with a little jelly. Put a few tiny pieces of broccoli and triangles of smoked salmon on top of each one and cover with more jelly. Leave in the fridge for 1–2 hours to set.

Put a little sea salt on each plate to help keep the oyster steady. You can also add a touch of blue food colouring to the salt to make it look like the sea.

Confit of wild salmon
with peas à la Française

The secret of success with this recipe is getting the duck fat or olive oil to the right temperature before you confit the salmon. If the fat is too hot, the salmon will be cooked on the outside but under-cooked inside.

1 litre olive oil or duck fat
4 x 200g wild salmon fillet, skinned

Peas à la Française
½ white onion, finely chopped
90g unsalted butter
1 tablespoon salt
600g fresh or frozen peas (podded weight)

100ml whipping cream
100g pancetta, cut into batons
2 baby gem lettuce, thinly sliced
salt and pepper

To make the pea purée

- Sweat the chopped onion in 50g of the butter for 4–5 minutes. Bring a pan of water to the boil and add 1 tablespoon of salt. Blanch the peas for 1–2 minutes and refresh in ice water. Drain, then add about one-third of the peas (about 200g) to the onions – keep the rest for the finished dish.

- Add the cream and seasoning to the peas and onions and cook together for a further 2 minutes. Blitz quickly and leave to chill – this helps keep the purée green until ready to serve.

To prepare the salmon

- Warm the oil or fat in a saucepan – the pan must be large enough to allow the salmon fillet to lie flat. Heat the oil or fat to 37°C – it should feel warm to your finger. Add the salmon and cook for 8–10 minutes, taking care that the temperature doesn't go above 37°C.

- Remove the salmon and slice it open to show the nice pink colour.

To finish the peas

- Blanch the pancetta in boiling water for 1 minute and then drain through a sieve. Sweat the bacon in the remaining 40g of butter, then add the rest of peas and the pea purée, and cook for 3–4 minutes. Add the lettuce, and check the seasoning.

To serve
Sprinkle the salmon fillet with sea salt and black pepper and serve on top of the peas.

Use a cooking thermometer to make sure you get the temperature of the fat or oil just right.

Lemon sole meunière

Serves 4

Lemon sole is delicious, but to make this dish extra special you could buy Dover sole, which is a lot more expensive but an outstanding fish. When cooking sole, use a good-quality, non-stick pan to get that lovely crispy golden colour.

4 x 450g lemon sole (on the bone)
3 tablespoons vegetable oil
30g flour

60g butter
2 lemons

- Remove the dark skin from the sole and scale the white skin. Then remove the heads and the fins with scissors. Wash and pat dry with kitchen paper.

- Heat the oil in a large pan. Quickly dust the sole in flour, tapping gently to remove any excess. Place the sole in the oil, white skin side down, and cook for about 4 minutes until golden. Turn the fish with a spatula and cook for a further 4 minutes, basting it with oil every 20 seconds. Cook the fish two at a time and keep in a warm place – you can put them in a hot oven very briefly before serving if necessary.

To serve
Serve the sole whole with wedges of lemon.

- When all the fish are cooked, pour off the oil from the pan, return the pan to the heat and add the butter. Cook the butter until it is light brown in colour (noisette) and add the juice of 1 lemon. Pour the butter and lemon over the fish.

Razor clams
with chorizo and lemon

If you can't get all the fresh herbs, I suggest you use the dill as that adds the most flavour.

1 carrot
1 courgette
100ml vegetable oil
100g broad beans (podded weight)
1 lemon
8 razor clams
2 shallots, peeled and finely chopped

100ml white wine
50g chorizo, finely diced
100ml whipping cream
50g chopped chives or parsley
knob of unsalted butter
salt and pepper

Garnish
bunch of chives, chopped
3 sprigs of dill, chopped
bunch of fresh amaranth leaves
2 sprigs of chervil, chopped

To prepare the vegetables

- Peel the carrot and cut into 5mm dice. Cut the green skin off the courgette and dice it – you don't need the white part for this recipe. Gently sauté the diced carrot and courgette in 1 teaspoon of vegetable oil for 3–4 minutes and set them aside.

- Remove the tough outer skin from the broad beans. Zest the lemon and squeeze the juice. Set both aside for later.

To prepare the razor clams

- Wash the razor clams well in cold running water, making sure you rinse away any sand and grit. Take a pan large enough to hold all the razor clams and place it over a high heat. Add the clams, shallots and white wine and immediately cover the pan with a tight-fitting lid so the clams steam. The razor clams should be cooked in 1 minute – don't be tempted to cook them any longer or they will become rubbery. Discard any clams that don't open.

- Remove the clams from their shells – keep the shells for serving. Slice the razor clam meat thinly at an angle around the brown intestine. Set aside.

- Reduce the white wine cooking liquor by half. Then add the chorizo, cream and the diced vegetables, broad beans and chopped chives or parsley while the liquid is simmering, stirring constantly. Once the cream thickens slightly, add the sliced razor clams, lemon juice and zest, and finish with a knob of butter.

To serve

Place some shells on each plate and pile in the razor clams, vegetables and creamy juices. Garnish with fresh herbs for decoration and added flavour.

Only buy live razor clams to be sure that
they are absolutely fresh.

Pan-fried calf's liver
with chicory and blood oranges

Serves 4

Liver is one of those things people either love or hate – I adore it. I now have few customers at the restaurant who ask in advance for special liver dishes because they know how much I enjoy cooking this type of food.

8 heads of chicory	olive oil	600g calf's liver
1 tablespoon butter	1 teaspoon fresh dill	2 tablespoons flour
2 blood oranges	1 teaspoon fresh chives	120ml veal jus or chicken
2 teaspoons honey	1 teaspoon fresh chervil	stock (see p.258)
1 teaspoon sherry vinegar	1 teaspoon fresh basil	

To serve
Place some of the braised chicory on each plate. Add the rested liver on top of the chicory and the salad on top of the liver. Warm the veal jus or chicken stock and pour around.

To prepare the braised chicory
- Trim off the bases of the chicory and separate the leaves. Set aside the middle leaves to use as a raw garnish. Cut the rest of the leaves into 5cm pieces for sautéing.

- Sauté the pieces of chicory in the butter, then add the grated zest of 1 blood orange and the honey. Deglaze the pan with a little splash of sherry vinegar and cook until the liquid has evaporated. Add the juice from the zested blood orange and cook gently for 15 minutes. The liquid will gradually reduce, concentrating all the delicious flavours together.

To prepare the chicory and blood orange salad
- Peel the remaining orange and cut it into large dice. Pick the herbs into small pieces and mix with the chicory leaves set aside earlier, the diced orange and a touch of olive oil.

To cook the calf's liver
- I like to serve calf's liver cut rather thicker than usual so it remains juicy and pink, like a good steak. Remove the outer skin from the liver and trim into 4 neat portions, taking care to remove any large veins.

- Heat a large frying pan and add 2 teaspoons of olive oil. Lightly dust the liver in flour and pan-fry for up to 4 minutes on each side. Leave to rest in a warm place for 3–4 minutes before serving.

Put the cut chicory into water and lemon juice to keep the colour and prevent it from going brown.

Rabbit
with macaroni and mustard sauce

Ask your butcher to de-bone the rabbit saddle, keeping the skin attached. Keep the bones – you will need them for the sauce. You will also need some giant macaroni tubes.

Rabbit
600g spinach
olive oil
1 garlic clove, chopped
1 shallot, peeled and finely chopped
4 saddles of rabbit
500g crepinette (caul fat)
salt and pepper
4 rabbit kidneys

Pasta
500g giant macaroni
50g butter
salt

Mustard sauce
20ml olive oil
4 rabbit bones
2 shallots, peeled and sliced
3 sprigs of tarragon
100ml brandy
750ml chicken stock
1 teaspoon grain mustard
1 carrot, finely diced
50g broad beans (podded woight)
1 spring onion, finely chopped

Béchamel sauce
60g butter
60g plain flour
1 litre of milk
4 gratings of nutmeg
50g grain mustard
salt and pepper

For serving
50g Parmesan cheese, grated

To prepare the rabbit

- Wash the spinach and dry it on kitchen towels. Heat a teaspoon of olive oil in a pan, add the spinach and garlic and cook until the spinach is wilted. Add the finely chopped shallot and cook for a further 2 minutes.

- Preheat the oven to 180°C/Gas 4. Lay the rabbit saddles flat on the crepinette and season with salt and pepper. Add the spinach mixture along the inside of the fillet on the skin side, then roll everything up like a spring roll and tie with kitchen string to secure tightly.

- Warm some olive oil in a pan and colour the rabbit until golden on all sides. Put into the oven and roast for 6–8 minutes until just cooked, adding the rabbit kidneys to the pan after the first 5 minutes. Take out of the oven and leave to rest in a warm place for 2–3 minutes.

You can make the béchamel up to two days in advance and keep it in the fridge. When ready to serve, warm a little milk in a pan, add the béchamel and whisk until you have a smooth sauce.

To make the mustard sauce

- Warm the olive oil in a heavy-bottomed pan. Chop the rabbit bones and add them to the pan. Cook until the bones start to caramelise – about 8–10 minutes. Add the sliced shallots and tarragon and sweat for another 3–4 minutes. Deglaze the pan with brandy and reduce until the pan is dry. Add the chicken stock and cook for 20 minutes. Pass the stock through a sieve, check seasoning and add the grain mustard, diced carrot, broad beans and spring onion.

To make the béchamel sauce

- In a medium saucepan, melt the butter and add the flour. Whisk over a low heat for 2–3 minutes until there are no lumps. Bring the milk to the boil with a little grated nutmeg and pour over the cooked roux. Bring to the boil and cook for 10 minutes, stirring gently. Season, pass through a sieve and stir in the grain mustard.

To cook the pasta

- Pour 500ml of water into a shallow roasting tray. Add the butter and salt and bring it to the boil. Add the macaroni to the water making sure they do not stick or break. Cook for 8–10 minutes until al dente. Once cooked, gently remove the pasta onto greaseproof paper and, while it is still warm, join the tubes together and cut to desired size. The macaroni will stick together naturally while warm.

To serve

Preheat the grill. Place the pasta on a tray and spoon over the béchamel sauce. Sprinkle with grated Parmesan and place under the grill until golden. Remove, cut into portions and place some on each plate. Trim the edges of the rabbit and place next to the pasta. Add a kidney on top and drizzle on the mustard sauce.

Rack of lamb
with braised spring lettuce parcels

Serves 4

Lettuce is delicious cooked. This is a method I learnt while working in the South of France and the subtle flavours of the lettuce go perfectly with the rack of lamb.

2 lamb racks	**Lettuce parcels**	1 onion, peeled and diced
2 tablespoons Dijon mustard	1 round lettuce, leaves separated	1 teaspoon herbes de Provence
1 bunch of chives, finely chopped	olive oil	1 bay leaf
100g podded fresh peas	2 baby gem lettuces	600ml lamb stock (see p.259)
100g podded broad beans	150g pancetta, cut in 1cm cubes	
salt and pepper	2 carrots, peeled and diced	

To serve

Warm the lettuce parcels in a pan together with the lettuce cooking liquid. Add the peas and the broad beans until cooked. Carve the racks into cutlets and serve with the lettuce parcels, peas and broad beans and the cooking liquid from the lettuce as a sauce.

To prepare the lettuce parcels

- Bring a large pan of salted water to the boil and briefly blanch the round lettuce leaves. Quickly refresh them in ice water, then remove with a slotted spoon and place on some kitchen paper to drain.

- Heat two tablespoons of olive oil in a frying pan. Cut the baby gem lettuces in half and place them in the pan, cut side down, to brown lightly. Remove the lettuces and set aside.

- Add a little more olive oil to the pan. Put in the pancetta, carrots, onion, herbes de Provence and bay leaves and cook slowly for 4–5 minutes over a low heat until nicely softened. Add the browned baby gem lettuces and the lamb stock, then cover and cook for another 5 minutes.

- Remove the lettuce hearts with a spatula. Pass the liquid through a sieve, keeping the diced vegetables for the lettuce parcels and the jus for the sauce. Place each half of baby gem lettuce on top of a blanched lettuce leaf with a teaspoon of the carrot and onion mixture, and wrap gently to form a parcel.

To cook the lamb

- Preheat the oven to 190°C/Gas 5. Heat a large heavy-bottomed frying pan with a tablespoon of olive oil. Season the lamb racks with salt and pepper and brown them in the pan on a high heat for about 2–3 minutes on each side until golden. Transfer to a roasting dish and roast in the preheated oven for another 6–8 minutes. Take the lamb out of the oven and leave to rest for 5 minutes on a cooling rack. Brush the racks with Dijon mustard and dip them in the chopped chives to coat.

A good chicken stock works just as well for this
recipe if you don't have lamb stock.

Shoulder of lamb
with garlic, fennel and rosemary roast potatoes

Serves 4

If you don't have fresh herbs, this recipe works well with dried herbes de Provence.

Ask the butcher to de-bone the shoulder as it can be quite tricky.

1 x 800g shoulder of lamb, boned
1 teaspoon ground cumin
1 teaspoon fennel seeds

4 sprigs fresh rosemary, chopped
3 tablespoons olive oil
2 fennel bulbs
320g new potatoes

12 garlic cloves, skin on
60g butter, diced
salt and pepper

To serve
Remove the string from the lamb and carve the meat into thin slices. Serve with the roasted vegetables and the cooking juices.

- Preheat the oven to 200°C/Gas 6. Open out the lamb shoulder and cover the meat with the cumin, fennel seeds, half the rosemary, salt and pepper. Roll into a large sausage and tie with string. Heat the oil in a heavy-bottomed frying pan, add the lamb and brown until golden all over. Set aside.

- Cut the fennel bulbs into quarters, trimming off any loose ends, and halve the new potatoes. Put the fennel, potatoes (cut side down) and garlic cloves into an ovenproof dish and sprinkle with the rest of the rosemary and the butter. Put the lamb on top of the vegetables and roast for 35 minutes. Remove and leave everything to rest for 15 minutes.

Beef tartare and carpaccio

As this dish is served raw, be sure to buy only the best quality meat. Also, be very conscious of hygiene when preparing the meat and make sure your work surfaces, equipment and cutting boards are all scrupulously clean.

160g rump of beef
4 quails' eggs

Mayonnaise and celeriac
1 egg yolk
1 teaspoon Dijon mustard
100ml vegetable oil
120g celeriac
chopped chives

Tartare dressing
2 egg yolks
2 teaspoons Dijon mustard
1 drop of Tabasco
1 teaspoon Worcester sauce
1 teaspoon tomato ketchup
1 teaspoon Cognac
200ml vegetable oil

1 teaspoon capers
1 teaspoon chopped gherkin
2 teaspoons chopped chives
2 teaspoons chopped parsley
salt and pepper

To serve
Mix the chopped beef and tartare dressing and shape into patties. Place one on each plate with a raw egg yolk on top. Place some celeriac topped with sliced beef alongside and serve with some soldiers of toast on the side if you wish.

To prepare the beef
- Remove any fat and sinew from the beef. Cut the rump in half and roll one half into a tight sausage. Wrap it in clingfilm and place in the freezer. Cut the other half of the rump into small dice and set aside until ready to serve.

- Once the rolled rump is frozen, slice it very thinly on a slicing machine if you have one. Alternatively, defrost the rump slightly and then carve with a very sharp knife. Arrange the slices neatly on oiled greaseproof paper.

To prepare the mayonnaise and celeriac
- Whisk together the egg yolk and mustard with a teaspoon of water. Slowly add the vegetable oil while continuing to whisk.

- Peel and finely dice the celeriac and blanch it in boiling water for about 30 seconds. Refresh in iced water, dry on a towel and mix with some of the mayonnaise and the chopped chives.

Tartare dressing
- Mix the egg yolks with the Dijon mustard. Add the Tabasco, Worcester sauce, ketchup and Cognac to taste. Slowly add the vegetable oil until the texture is like mayonnaise. Check the seasoning and add the capers, gherkins and chopped herbs.

Country terrine

You will need a large terrine or loaf tin.

125g butter
400g onions, peeled and
  chopped
2 garlic cloves, finely
  chopped
salt

100ml brandy
1 teaspoon dried thyme
pinch of ground cloves
1 teaspoon juniper berries
1 teaspoon ground mace

800g pork fat
1kg pigs' liver
2 eggs
450g streaky bacon

- Heat a frying pan and add the butter. Sweat the onions and garlic gently in the butter over medium heat until very soft. Season with salt. Add the brandy, thyme and spices and cook for a further 5 minutes. Leave to cool on a plate.

- Mince the pork fat and then the liver and combine with the onion mixture. Add the eggs and stir in well.

- Preheat the oven to 150°C/Gas 2. Line the terrine with clingfilm and lay the streaky bacon over the clingfilm in overlapping layers. Leave enough bacon hanging over the edges so it can be folded over the top of the terrine.

- Pour the pork mixture into the terrine. Fold the bacon over the top and then cover with the clingfilm. Gently pierce a few holes in the top and cover with a piece of aluminium foil. Place the terrine in a roasting pan and pour in boiling water to come halfway up the sides. Place in the oven and cook for 1 hour and 20 minutes.

To serve

Take the terrine out of the water bath, but do not unmould. Once cool, leave the terrine in the fridge overnight to set properly. Slice when ready and serve with gherkins, home-made chutney and bread. This terrine keeps for a week in the fridge.

Boned and rolled chicken
stuffed with spinach and asparagus

This recipe does involve quite a few stages of preparation, but don't let that put you off as it is well worth the effort. You will need some butcher's string and a trussing needle.

1 free-range chicken
4 spears of asparagus
1 teaspoon olive oil
200g cooked spinach
1 teaspoon vegetable oil
50g unsalted butter
1 shallot, peeled and finely
  chopped

4 garlic cloves, peeled
4 young carrots

Sauce
1 teaspoon vegetable oil
1 chicken carcass,
  chopped small
3 shallots, peeled and
  chopped

2 tomatoes, chopped
1 sprig of tarragon
skin of 1 lemon (use a
  vegetable peeler)
3 garlic cloves, peeled
50ml brandy
50ml Noilly Prat

- Turn the chicken breast side down and cut down the centre of the bird. Using a sharp knife, remove the breast meat and legs from the carcass, being careful not to pierce the skin. Place your index finger and thumb around the wishbone and hold the skin down with your other hand. Pull the carcass and it will come away from the skin. Remove the legs, breasts and wing bones until you are left with only the skin, which can now be cut in half.

- Heat the olive oil in a saucepan and add the asparagus spears. Season and cook over a medium heat for 4 or 5 minutes until softened but still crunchy. Set them aside.

- Wash and dry the spinach. Wilt the spinach in a hot pan with a teaspoon of vegetable oil and a pinch of salt for about 2 minutes until very soft. Drain it in a sieve, pressing with a spoon to squeeze out excess water, then set aside to cool for 3–4 minutes.

- Melt the butter in a large pan over medium heat. Add the finely chopped shallot and cook for 2–3 minutes. Then add the spinach. Mix thoroughly, season and set aside to cool.

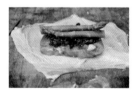

- Lay 1 chicken breast on the skin and place half the spinach on top with 2 asparagus spears. Meanwhile, separate the chicken leg from the thigh and remove the bone from the leg taking care to remove all the sinew. Place on top of the asparagus.

Keep the juices left in the foil after the chicken has rested and use them as a sauce.

Pull the chicken skin over and truss from one end to the other with butcher's string and a trussing needle. Make a second parcel in the same way.

To make the chicken jus

Heat the oil in a heavy-bottomed pan until smoking. Add the chopped chicken carcass and cook for 6–8 minutes, turning frequently until golden brown.

Add the shallots, tomatoes, tarragon, lemon rind and garlic. Cook for a further 3–4 minutes. Next pour in the brandy and Noilly Prat and reduce until almost dry. Now pour over just enough water to cover the carcass and cook for 20 minutes. Strain through a fine sieve and reduce by half. Set aside.

To finish the dish

Preheat the oven to 200°C/Gas 6. In an ovenproof pan, heat a teaspoon of vegetable oil and gently brown the carrots. Season and add the cloves of garlic. Place in the oven for 10–12 minutes.

Season the stuffed chicken. Heat a teaspoon of oil in a large non-stick pan and gently brown the chicken until golden. This will take about 6 minutes. Place the chicken in the oven and roast for 6 minutes, then turn and roast for another 6 minutes. Remove from the oven, wrap in foil and leave to rest for 10 minutes.

Once properly rested, cut each end off the chicken and carefully pull the trussing string out. It should come out easily in one piece.

To serve

Slice the chicken, place it on warmed plates and serve with the roasted carrots and garlic and the chicken juices.

Blood oranges

Prepare the sponges the day before you are going to eat them and serve at room temperature. You will need four metal moulds measuring 7.5cm across.

Dried orange slices
4–5 blood oranges, peeled and divided into segments
100g icing sugar

Oatmeal sponge
125g softened butter plus 30g for greasing moulds

125g honey
3 whole eggs
75g ground almonds
50g oatmeal, fine or medium grain
30g plain flour
15ml whisky

Blood orange cream
2 whole eggs
75g sugar
zest and juice from 2 blood oranges
juice of ½ lemon
125g unsalted butter
1 leaf gelatin

To serve
Place a spoonful of blood orange cream on each plate and top with an unmoulded oatmeal sponge. Arrange some dried orange segments on top of the sponge.

To make the dried orange slices
- Place the blood orange segments on a baking tray lined with greaseproof paper. Dust with icing sugar, then turn the slices over and dust the other side. Place in a very low oven (100°C/Gas ½) for 1½–2 hours, then check. Set aside to cool at room temperature.

To make the oatmeal sponge
- Preheat the oven to 180°C/Gas 4. Butter the moulds with the 30g of softened butter and set aside. Mix the 125g of butter with the honey until smooth. Gradually mix in the eggs one at a time. In a separate bowl, mix together the almonds, oatmeal and flour in a separate bowl.

- Pour the almond mixture into the butter, honey and eggs and fold together until well mixed. Stir in the whisky. Pour the sponge into the greased moulds and bake in the preheated oven for 20 minutes until golden brown. Leave the sponges to cool before unmoulding.

To make the blood orange cream
- Mix the eggs, sugar and the blood orange zest and juice with the lemon juice in a metal mixing bowl. Melt the butter in a pan – do not allow it to boil. Add the butter to the mixing bowl. Place the bowl over a pan of simmering water and whisk gently for 20 minutes or until the mixture thickens enough to coat the back of a spoon.

- Meanwhile soak the gelatin in a small bowl of cold water for 5 minutes. Squeeze out the excess water and add the gelatin to the blood orange cream mixture.

- Mix well and place in fridge for 2–3 hours to set slightly.

If you don't want to use alcohol in this recipe, add
freshly squeezed orange juice instead of whisky.

Crêpes
with cherries

Although these crêpes are best when freshly cooked, they can be stored in an airtight container for up to three days in the fridge or two months in the freezer.

Crêpe batter
200ml water
3 whole eggs
120g flour
60ml melted butter

1 tablespoon caster sugar
pinch salt
1 teaspoon vegetable oil
    for greasing the pan

Cherry sauce
100g caster sugar
100g butter
50ml kirsch
300g fresh cherries,
    stones removed

To serve
Fold the crêpes and warm them through in the cherry sauce so that they absorb the sauce. Serve the crêpes topped with cherry sauce.

To make the crêpes
- Mix all the ingredients for the batter in a bowl and whisk until smooth. Allow the batter to rest for one hour at room temperature.

- Heat a small non-stick frying pan with a ¼ of a teaspoon of vegetable oil. Pour in a small ladleful of batter and swirl about to spread evenly. Cook for 30 seconds and flip. Cook for another 10 seconds and remove. Lay the crêpe out flat so it can cool. Repeat the process until all the batter is used up.

To prepare the cherry sauce
- Put the caster sugar in a heavy-bottomed pan over medium heat and cook gently until golden. Remove the pan from heat, add the butter and mix with a wooden spoon until completely melted.

- Place the pan back on the heat and add the kirsch. Ignite with a match or lighter and flambé. Allow the flame to burn out and the liquid to reduce slightly. Add the cherries and continue to cook until the fruit is just soft and liquid has reduced enough to coat the back of a spoon.

Always take great care with the flambé technique
so that nothing catches fire.

Citrus fruit and Earl Grey jelly
with Earl Grey sorbet

I was inspired to try using tea as an infusion in desserts after I enjoyed some refreshing iced tea recently. In this recipe I have used Earl Grey tea, but jasmine or green tea works well too.

Jelly
2½ leaves of gelatin
juice of 8 oranges
5 Earl Grey teabags
50g sugar
2 oranges
2 blood oranges
2 pink grapefruit
2 white grapefruit
2 limes
handful of fresh mint

Sorbet
30ml water
80g sugar
4 Earl Grey teabags
400ml orange juice (6–8
    oranges)
150ml pink grapefruit juice

To serve
Remove the jellies from the fridge and wipe around the rim of the dishes to remove condensation. Add a scoop of sorbet to the middle of each jelly.

To make the jelly

- Soak the gelatin leaves in water for 3–4 minutes until soft, then squeeze out the excess water. Pour the orange juice into a saucepan and gently warm until simmering. Add the teabags and the sugar – if the oranges are a bit sour, add a little more sugar. Whisk in the gelatin. Leave to infuse for 5 minutes, then pass through a fine sieve. Leave the liquid to cool in the fridge for 10–15 minutes.

- Meanwhile, peel and segment the oranges, grapefruit and limes. Pour the cooled liquid on top of the citrus segments in the serving bowls, making sure all the fruit is covered. Cut the mint leaves into fine strips and sprinkle them over the jelly. Leave the jelly in the fridge to set – about 1½–2 hours.

To make the sorbet

- Put the water and sugar into a pan, bring to the boil and add the teabags. Stir in the orange and grapefruit juice, then pass through a fine sieve. Freeze in an ice cream machine.

If you don't fancy making the sorbet yourself,
use a good-quality bought sorbet.

Rice pudding
with grapes

I often serve this rice pudding with grapes, but it is delicious with any seasonal fruit compote.

500ml whole milk
100g short-grain rice
60g caster sugar
1 vanilla pod, split
    lengthwise
1 leaf of gelatin

130ml whipping cream
65ml natural yoghurt
30g golden raisins
200g green grapes
200g red grapes

Sauternes syrup
375ml Sauternes
1 vanilla pod, split
    lengthwise
4 sticks liquorice
50g caster sugar
juice of 1 lemon

For the rice pudding

- Place the milk, rice, sugar and vanilla in a heavy-bottomed saucepan and bring to a simmer over medium heat. Then turn heat down to low and leave the rice to cook gently for 30 minutes or until it is soft and most of the liquid is absorbed.

- Soak the gelatin leaf in cold water for 5 minutes and squeeze out excess moisture. Add to the warm rice mixture. Transfer the rice to a wide bowl and leave to cool.

- Whisk the cream to firm peaks and mix with the yoghurt. Once the rice is cool, fold in the yoghurt mixture and add the raisins. Pour the rice pudding mixture into individual moulds and leave to set in the fridge for at least 45–60 minutes before serving. Cut the grapes in half and set aside.

To prepare the Sauternes syrup

- Place the Sauternes, vanilla pod, liquorice, sugar and lemon juice into a saucepan and bring to the boil. Allow the syrup to boil until the liquid has reduced enough to coat the back of a spoon. Pour the syrup through a fine sieve and set aside. Save the liquorice sticks for the garnish.

To serve

Warm the halved red and green grapes in a saucepan with the Sauternes syrup. Unmould the rice puddings and place one on each plate. Serve with warmed grapes and Sauternes sauce and decorate with a liquorice stick.

Poached rhubarb
with cheesecake mousse

Serves 4

I cooked a version of this recipe in the final of Great British Menu on BBC in spring 2009 and it proved a hit with the judges and my fellow contestants.

Crowdie cheesecake mousse
450g Crowdie cheese
125g sugar
1½ tablespoons flour
1 tablespoon vanilla extract
zest of 1 lemon
1 egg
1 egg yolk

Rhubarb
3 sticks of rhubarb
400g sugar
juice and zest of 1 lemon

Jelly
200ml reserved poaching liquid
2 sheets or 4g gelatin

Crumble
75g oats
75g pecans
1 teaspoon egg whites
1 tablespoon icing sugar

Garnish
4 sprigs lemon thyme

To serve
Place 4 or 5 rhubarb strips on each plate, slightly overlapping one another. Scoop out a portion of the cheesecake mousse, place on top and wrap a rhubarb strip around it. Add a small spoonful of rhubarb purée and some slices of rhubarb jelly beside the mousse. Sprinkle over the crumble and garnish with a sprig of lemon thyme and any reserved poaching syrup you may have left.

To make the cheesecake mousse
- Preheat the oven to 150°C/Gas 2. Put the cheese, sugar, flour, vanilla and lemon zest in a blender and mix until smooth. In a separate jug, mix the egg and egg yolk together, then pour into the blender with the cheese mixture and blend again until smooth.

- Pour into a 23cm baking dish and cover with aluminium foil. Bake for 35–40 minutes until set. Allow to cool and then transfer the mixture to a blender and blitz until smooth. Leave this to set in the fridge for at least 1 hour before serving.

To prepare the rhubarb carpaccio
- Cut 2 of the sticks of rhubarb into pieces about 10cm long. Using a mandolin or a very sharp knife, slice these rhubarb pieces into 3mm strips and set aside.

- Place the sugar, lemon zest and juice into a saucepan with 600ml of water and bring to the boil, then remove from the heat. Put the rhubarb strips into a bowl and pour the hot syrup over them. Leave the rhubarb to cook in the hot syrup for 5 minutes until just soft. Remove the rhubarb, lay it out on a plate, then put in the fridge to cool. Keep the syrup for later.

To prepare the rhubarb purée
- Chop the remaining rhubarb stick finely and place in a small bowl. Put the syrup, set aside when making the carpaccio, back to the boil, then pour it over chopped rhubarb. Cover the bowl with clingfilm and leave the rhubarb for about 10 minutes until soft. Strain it through a sieve, saving the poaching syrup for making the jelly. Blitz the rhubarb with a hand blender or mash it with a fork to make a smooth purée.

To make the rhubarb jelly

Bring the poaching syrup to the boil, then take it off the heat. Soak the gelatin in a bowl of cold water for 5 minutes, squeeze out excess moisture and add to poaching liquid. Mix well, pour into a mould and leave to set in the fridge.

To prepare the crumble mix

Preheat the oven to 180*C/Gas 4. Toss all the ingredients together and spread out evenly on a lined baking tray. Bake for 6–8 minutes until golden brown. Leave to cool, then mix with your hands to create the crumble texture.

You can use Philadelphia cream cheese instead of Scottish Crowdie.

Apple beignets
with cider sabayon and vanilla ice cream

Serves 4

When I was a child we used to pick apples in autumn to store through the winter. Come spring, my nana used to make these delicious beignets to use up the last ones.

2 Granny Smith apples
30g flour
500ml of vegetable oil (to fry the beignets)

Sabayon
3 egg yolks
50g sugar
300ml cider

Vanilla ice cream
5 egg yolks
130g caster sugar
250ml milk
250ml whipping cream
1 vanilla pod, split lengthwise

Beignet batter
8 egg yolks
500g flour
500ml cider
8 egg whites
100g icing sugar

To serve
Drain the apple beignets on paper towels to remove any excess fat and dust them with icing sugar. Serve with vanilla ice cream and a generous spoon of the cider sabayon.

To make the vanilla ice cream

- Using a whisk, beat the egg yolks with the sugar in a bowl until pale and slightly thickened. Meanwhile heat the milk, cream and vanilla to a simmer and set aside.

- In a heavy-bottomed pan, warm the beaten eggs and sugar over a very low heat, stirring constantly. Gradually stir in the hot milk mix. Cook over a low heat, stirring with a wooden spoon until the mixture thickens just enough to coat the back of the spoon. Take off the heat and discard the vanilla pod. Strain the custard through a sieve into a large bowl and then set over a bowl of ice water to cool. Pour into an ice cream machine and churn. Churn until just frozen, then place into an airtight plastic container and freeze for at least 3 hours before serving.

To make the sabayon

- Whisk the egg yolks and sugar together in a metal bowl over a pan of simmering water. Whisk until the mixture becomes slightly frothy, then slowly pour in cider. Keep whisking until the sauce thickens – this will take at least 10 minutes.

- The sabayon can be served at this stage but if you would like to serve it cool, take the pan off the heat and whisk the sabayon until it is room temperature. At this point you can set the sabayon aside and prepare the rest of the dish.

To make the beignets

- Whisk the yolks with the cider and slowly add the flour until completely mixed. In a separate bowl, whisk the egg whites to firm peaks and fold into the cider mix.

- Peel and core apples, keeping them whole. Cut each apple into 4 doughnut-shaped slices, about 0.5cm thick. Pour the vegetable oil into a large pan and heat to 170–180°C. Dust the apple pieces with flour to coat and dip them into beignet batter. Cook the dipped apple pieces in oil until golden brown on each side. Use a wooden skewer to help with the flipping and removing of the finished beignets.

If you don't have a thermometer for the fryer, drop a spoonful of batter into the fryer to check if it is hot enough.

Summer

Summer should be a celebration of simplicity and I like to let summer produce speak for itself. In simple dishes, such as cold vegetable soups or artichokes served with rustic bread and a vinaigrette sauce, the textures, flavours and summer freshness of the ingredients go together beautifully. I appreciate that simple food can mean different things to different people, but for me it's all about respecting the produce and maximising its natural potential to get the best results. I try to drum this into my guys in the kitchen every day – respect your produce! If you don't respect the produce, nobody will respect your cooking.

For me, cooking is about recognising and appreciating food and relying on your own instincts by touching or smelling the produce. Appreciate the natural flavours of summer food and enjoy the juiciness of the fruits and berries, the freshness of summer vegetables. Let your imagination flow to create new and exciting dishes with whatever is around you and keep the food miles to a minimum whenever possible. The fruit and berries from the fields and woods in Scotland are of outstanding quality. Although vegetables can be slightly harder to find due to the climate, I rely on the smaller growers, such as Robin on the Isle of Arran who uses seaweed to fertilise the soil. His vegetables are fantastic. Whenever I am experimenting with new dishes or looking for new taste combinations, I look at the many matches Nature itself makes. Berries and vegetables used with fresh fish or meat; courgette flowers with langoustines; summer lettuce with rabbit – all ingredients used the way nature intended

Honey is a great example of this. Honey in the summer is outstanding, and one of my favourites is the heather honey we get from a honey farm in Perthshire. The bees gather nectar and pollen from the heather on the surrounding hills and the flavour comes through in the honey itself. I adore honey with my summer desserts, particularly with raspberries, elderflowers or gooseberries to maximise the natural flavours. The quality of the Scottish strawberries, blueberries, brambles (or blackberries) is truly outstanding in mid-July when they are in their prime, and they work so well together.

I am particularly proud to get most of my berries from Blairgowrie in Perthshire. The unique balance of rain and the fertility of the soil make this an ideal climate for growing berries. In Scotland, one of the reasons we're not able to get the vegetables and berries earlier in the season than we do is due to the fact that we don't have such severe frosts anymore. This has a tremendous impact on the fruit and berries in just the same way as vineyards rely on the right weather conditions for the best grapes.

To me, the courgette flower is another symbol of summer and I've used these ever since I first discovered their beauty. The courgette flower is something many people in Scotland have in their

gardens but don't know how to use in cooking. Stuffed with a ratatouille of vegetables or fresh langoustines and blanched in hot oil, courgette flowers are transformed into crispy, flavourful beauties. The flavours and textures are a delight and perfectly in tune with the taste of summer.

Franck Cerutti, head chef at Le Louis XV, and Pierre Koffmann are both great masters of simple flavours. Trying to use too many flavours together easily confuses the palate and over-shadows the taste sensation. In my early days at La Tante Claire, one of my jobs was to prepare Chef's dinner every night. I was only 19 and it was quite a daunting job so I often relied on the guidance of the older chefs to get it right. Not only does Koffmann have one of the most respected palates in the trade, but also his whole presence made me want to push myself so as not to disappoint him. Koffmann was often on a so-called-diet and pretty specific about his dinner requests. His 6 o'clock meal had to be tasty but simple, and he wanted a new dish every day.

I remember one day we had just received some impressive John Dory in the kitchen, and Chef told me to come up with some ideas for his dinner. I was young and saw my chance to impress so started creating a dish in my head. I was thinking about wrapping the fish and steaming it. My mind was busy with ideas for lots of flavours – herbs, a garlic cream, ravioli, some kind of crisps – but I was soon warned to keep it simple.

'Don't mess with beautiful produce,' Koffmann told me. 'Keep the fish as it comes, grill it, add some lemon and olive oil and serve it on a bed of wilted young spinach. Simple! You must master the basics of cooking before taking it to the next level!'

As a young chef, I was over-complicating things without knowing the basics and this is something I believe is done by many chefs today. One of many

things Koffmann taught me was how to discover the beauty of the basics and to learn about my own palate. This is incredibly important advice for any chef or cook. Know your basics and taste everything you cook! Think about flavours when you eat, what goes together in your mouth, what doesn't. Reflect on textures as they hit your tongue. Don't mix too many flavours on the plate as this will only confuse your

palate and take away the sensation of other flavours. During my years at La Tante Claire, I was always told if food was too salty, not salty enough, or not cooked to perfection – believe me! Some days Chef told me he wouldn't even serve my food to his dogs. Other days he'd give me a hard squeeze on the shoulder, which was as good as it gets and the only way of knowing that he had enjoyed it.

I do, however, believe that simplicity is linked with confidence in cooking. I feel that there is an urge for today's young chefs to strive for visual beauty on the plate, rather than focusing on flavours and keeping the food simple. For me, cooking is all about the flavours and textures in my dishes. Taste sensations

are the key. Of course you want your dish to look attractive and appealing, but that comes afterwards. Get your cooking right and then think about how to present it on a plate. Don't attempt to do it the other way round – it will never work.

A tip when dressing your plate is once again to refer to the origin of your produce. Garnish your meat with herbs of the season or only ever use an accompanying sauce or purée from vegetables that grow where your meat comes from, again in season. Keep the ingredients in perfect harmony, looking simple but stunning on the plate.

I love the traditions of enjoying big feasts – everything laid out on the table and everyone tucking in together. For me, enjoying a meal is as much about socialising as the food – talking about the food, discussing the wines, reflecting on the day. In my case, the best chance of catching up with my friends is over a good meal. As a chef, it's not always easy for me to find time to see friends, but I try to make up for it by cooking them a good meal. They always appreciate it (although they sometimes think I am crazy for wanting to cook on my day off), but for me it's the ideal evening. Good food and great friends – what more could you want! For obvious reasons I suppose it's easier to hold gatherings in the summer months because of the longer, lighter days, but there is always such pleasure in sharing a dinner table with people who are just as excited about what they're eating as I am. Sadly, I know that some people have never experienced this, as the habit of sharing a family meal around the dinner table is slowly disappearing in many households.

Sometimes in summer evenings, I go out picking elderflowers, which grow wild all around Scotland. My wife has picked elderflowers since childhood and makes a fantastic elderflower cordial, which we often drink in the summer, or make into a sorbet when having friends over. Elderflowers are so much fun to pick and they are easy to find.

Most shellfish are at their prime in the summer, in mid-July. The waters have warmed up, the langoustines have cast their shells by burying themselves in the sand. The scallops, lobsters and crabs are all in their prime and so are many kinds of fish. What can possibly taste better than newly caught fish or shellfish prepared and cooked in a matter of hours?

When you're buying fish, take a good look at them before you make your choice. Massage the fish gently, feel it with your fingers if you can and make sure the gills are shining and the eyes are clear. Check that the scales have a beautiful shimmer. Don't leave the fish sitting in its own juices – ice it, wrap it up and cook it as soon as you get home. Most fishmongers are helpful if you ask them to get you something special. I love to try some of the unusual fish and shellfish from the Scottish shores. Razor clams and sea urchins, for example, are not only cheaper than some of the more familiar seafood but they also taste magnificent and they look great on the plate!

Good food tastes that wee bit better when eaten outdoors. I've often asked myself why this is and I've come to the conclusion that it's to do with being in the fresh air and in the middle of nature. You can take in the smells, aromas and sounds of nature while tucking into good, simple food. Summer is about enjoying barbecues, dinner in the garden, picnics in the woods or by the ocean, giving you the chance to re-charge your batteries before the darker months.

Elderflower cordial

Elderflowers (fresh or dried) can be used to make not only delicious cordial but also tea and jam, and they can be added to rhubarb and gooseberries as a spice. This cordial keeps well in the fridge for a few months, or you can store it in an airtight container in the freezer for six months or longer. It doesn't set once frozen and stays sorbet-like in texture so is ideal for adding a unique taste to a summer cocktail.

The berries of the elderflower plant also make good jelly and chutney. Always remember that only the flowers and the berries of the elderflower tree can be used in cooking. The leaves and bark are poisonous.

40–50 elderflowers
4 5 organic unwaxed lemons

1.75kg sugar
60g ascorbic acid

To serve
You can simply dilute the cordial with still or sparkling water. Alternatively, add a teaspoon of frozen cordial to a glass of champagne or a tablespoon to white wine for a refreshing drink.

- Pick the elderflowers, choosing ones that are in full bloom, with no bugs!

- Bring a litre of water to the boil and meanwhile cut the lemons into thin slices. Put the lemon slices, elderflowers, sugar and ascorbic acid into a large container and pour in the boiling water. Mix well.

- Cover and leave in the fridge for five days, stirring occasionally. Then strain, pour into sterilised glass bottles and store in the fridge.

Globe artichokes

Once you have enjoyed the leaves of the artichoke and only the heart remains, gently cut away the hairs and eat the delicious heart with the vinaigrette dressing.

4 artichokes
2 tablespoons lemon juice

Vinaigrette
1 tablespoon Dijon mustard
1 tablespoon white wine
vinegar
200ml vegetable oil
salt and pepper

To serve
Serve the artichokes warm with the vinaigrette dressing alongside. Gently remove the leaves one at a time and dip them in the dressing before eating.

Preparing the artichokes
- Remove the tough outer leaves of the artichokes and snap off the stalks. Carefully trim off the top spiky leaves with a sharp knife and discard.

- Bring a large pan of water to the boil – do not use aluminium or iron pans as they can cause the artichokes to discolour. Add the lemon juice, then the artichokes. A useful tip is to put an old plate on top of the artichokes to keep them submerged so they cook evenly. Simmer, uncovered, for 30–40 minutes, or until one of the outer leaves pulls away easily. Drain well.

Making the vinaigrette
- Mix the mustard and vinegar in a bowl using a hand whisk. Gently pour in the oil and mix with a hand blender until the vinaigrette is properly emulsified. As it thickens, add about 50ml water and taste for seasoning.

Basil sorbet

A sorbet is a wonderful dish to serve in summer, either to excite the taste buds at the beginning of a meal or refresh the palate between courses. A beautifully fresh green basil sorbet can be served on its own or added to gazpacho as shown overleaf. The flavours of basil and tomato are perfectly in tune and are a real taste of summer.

300g caster sugar
100g fresh basil
juice of 3 limes

- Put the sugar and 600ml of water in a pan and bring to the boil. Take the pan off the heat, set the syrup aside to cool and then chill in the fridge.

- Put the basil leaves and chilled syrup into a blender and blitz until smooth – don't blend for any longer than you need or the mixture will get too warm and lose its bright green colour. Sieve and then transfer the mixture to an ice cream machine. While it is churning, add the lime juice and continue to churn until frozen. Store in a freezer until needed.

- If you don't have an ice cream machine, pour the mixture into a tray and freeze. Six to eight times during the freezing process take the mixture out and stir until ice crystals start to form. Fluff again with a fork before serving.

To serve

Run a dessertspoon under warm water, spoon out some sorbet and shape into a neat quenelle. Place in a glass or on top of a bowl of chilled gazpacho.

Adding lime juice during churning helps keep the sorbet a wonderful bright green colour.

Gazpacho

I add a sugar and vinegar mixture called a gastrique to my gazpacho. Gastriques are great in tomato dishes and sauces, as they balance the acidity of the tomato.

10 tomatoes	**Basil-infused olive oil**	**Garnish**
½ fennel bulb	500ml olive oil	red pepper, chopped
2 large red peppers, seeds removed	12 basil stalks	tomato, peeled and diced
2 celery sticks		spring onion, chopped
1 large shallot, peeled	**Gastrique**	yellow pepper, chopped
⅔ cucumber, skin on	100g sugar	1 tablespoon olive oil
2 tablespoons tomato purée	100ml white wine vinegar	basil sorbet (see p.101)
1 tablespoon sherry vinegar (or to taste)		fresh basil leaves
salt and pepper		black pepper

To serve

Freeze your bowls before serving so the gazpacho stays cold. Place some sautéed garnish in the middle of a shallow bowl and pour the gazpacho around it. Add a spoonful of basil sorbet on top and garnish with a few basil leaves and a twist of black pepper.

Basil-infused oil

- Start by making the basil-infused olive oil. Warm the oil and add the basil stalks. Leave to infuse overnight.

Gastrique

- Put the sugar and vinegar into a pan and bring to the boil. Cook until the sugar is fully dissolved.

To make the gazpacho

- Chop the tomatoes roughly – there's no need to skin or seed them. Remove the core and tough outer leaves from the fennel and chop roughly with the peppers, celery, shallot and cucumber. Put all the vegetables into a blender or food processor with the tomato purée, sherry vinegar, basil oil, gastrique and seasoning. Blitz until smooth. Keep the finished gazpacho in the fridge for at least 2 hours before serving so it is well chilled and the flavours are more intense. Check the seasoning.

To prepare the garnish

- Lightly sauté the vegetables in a pan with the olive oil for 2–3 minutes until lightly wilted. Set aside and leave to cool until ready to serve.

Make the gazpacho a day in advance if you can so
the flavours have time to intensify.

Few things taste better in the summer than sautéed mushrooms on toast. I used to eat this at my nana's house when I was younger and to this day I always make sure I go out mushrooming a few times a year. I love being out in the woods in the summer, especially on a sunny day. We prepare a picnic, bring along a good bottle of Bandol and make a day of it. If I am lucky, my fungi forager comes with us and shows us the best places.

The best time for finding mushrooms is after a rainy spell followed by a day or two of sunshine – ideal growing conditions. Mushrooms tend to grow in the same spot every year, so if you've found a good place, remember it and make a point of going back there. Girolles, in particular, tend to grow in circles – if you find one, you're almost sure to find a few more nearby. When foraging for mushrooms, stick to picking the ones you're 100 per cent sure of. Take a good up-to-date field guide with you and check with an expert if you're worried. Don't take any chances – there are many kinds of very poisonous mushrooms.

Girolles are my personal favourites and they're relatively easy to find and recognise by their yellow hats and the spores underneath. They usually grow in birch and beech woods and I love trying to spot them. I always use a clean, sharp knife to cut the stem at ground level, as I believe new girolles will grow better if not uprooted.

By late June I can usually expect my trusted forager to arrive at the restaurant with the first girolles. Or even better, I put my wellies on, gather the family and a few friends, my treasured mushroom basket

and my mother's beloved dog Rio and go out in search of girolles myself. When I recently suggested a fungi foraging trip to our London friends Jon and Anniken as something to do during their weekend stay in Scotland, they just laughed and thought I was joking. Of course I wasn't, and a few hours later they were hooked and asked to come up for the next mushroom hunt.

> When foraging for mushrooms, stick to picking the ones you're 100 per cent sure of. Don't take any chances.

Preparing the girolles

Here's the best way to prepare girolles for using in the recipe on page 106 and others. Clean and trim the girolles carefully. Submerge them briefly in cold water and mix thoroughly to remove any dirt and grit. Drain them well.

Heat some vegetable oil in a heavy-bottomed frying pan and slowly sauté the girolles over a low heat. Season with half a teaspoon of salt, then cover the pan with a lid and slowly leave the mushrooms to braise in the juices they release as they cook. Strain the girolles and keep the liquid as it makes an excellent stock to use in soup, gravies and other dishes. The liquid can be frozen and taken out to use when needed.

Scottish girolles on toast
with poached eggs and chorizo

1 teaspoon vegetable oil
300g girolles, cooked
    (see p.105)
10 flat-leaf parsley leaves
2 sprigs of thyme, plus
    extra for garnish

1 tablespoon chopped
    chives
2 shallots, finely chopped
2 garlic cloves
100g chorizo, cut into thin
    strips

4 slices baguette or other
    thick crusty bread
olive oil
100ml white wine vinegar
4 eggs
salt and pepper

To serve
Put some sautéed
mushroom mix on each
slice of toast and top
with a poached egg.
Sprinkle over a few leaves
of thyme and a twist of
black pepper.

To prepare the mushrooms
- Heat a frying pan and add the vegetable oil. Add the girolles and cook them until golden. Then add the parsley, thyme, chives, shallots and 1 finely sliced garlic clove. Lastly mix in the chorizo and season with salt and pepper to taste.

- Meanwhile, grill the bread till crisp and rub with the other garlic clove, cut in half. Drizzle with olive oil.

To poach the eggs
- Bring a large pan of water to the boil. Add the vinegar and stir to create a whirlpool effect. Crack each egg into a separate cup, then pour the eggs into the water and poach for about 3 minutes.

- Remove the eggs from the pan with a slotted spoon and drain well.

Wash mushrooms as little as possible as
they absorb water and lose their flavour.

Roast bone marrow
with snails and parsley salad

I serve this dish with a parsley salad that balances the richness of the bone marrow and the snails. Andrew Hogg, of South West Snails, is our supplier. His snails are reared indoors so there's no grit to be removed. The snails have, however, been washed four or five times in the week before they arrive at the restaurant so their digestive systems are completely clean.

1kg organic snails
200g girolles, cooked
  (see p.105)
2 marrow bones, each
  10cm long, split
  lengthwise
1 teaspoon butter
1 teaspoon marjoram
  leaves
1 teaspoon shallots,
  chopped
1 teaspoon chives,
  chopped
salt and pepper

Snail stock
2 carrots, peeled
2 onions
2 celery sticks
7 star anise
5 cardamom pods,
  crushed
1 teaspoon fennel seeds
1 leek
3 tablespoons salt
parsley stalks

Chlorophyll
1 bunch flat-leaf parsley

Garlic sauce
10–15 garlic cloves, peeled
350ml whipping cream

Shallot and parsley salad
1 small bunch of flat-leaf
  parsley, leaves picked
  from stems (use stems
  for stock)
2 shallots, sliced into rings
1 teaspoon capers
1 tablespoon olive oil
lemon juice
salt and pepper

To make the stock and cook the snails
- Bring a large pan of water to the boil. Peel and chop the carrots and onions and add them to the pan with the rest of the stock ingredients. Bring back to the boil. Add the snails, lower the heat to medium and simmer for 4–5 hours until the snails are tender. Don't let the liquid boil as that will make the snails tough. Once the snails are cooked, leave them to rest in the stock off the heat for another hour. Remove the snails from the shells with a skewer and separate the edible sections from the intestines. Throw the intestines away and set the snails aside.

To make the chlorophyll
- Place the parsley and 1.5 litres of water in a blender and blitz for 5 minutes until very smooth and green. Strain through a fine sieve and pour the strained liquid into a saucepan. Throw away the leftover pulp in the sieve. Slowly heat the liquid over a low flame until a soft raft forms as the green particles start to cling to one another. Skim this mixture into a muslin-lined sieve and let it drain naturally for 30 minutes. Gently squeeze out any excess moisture. Scrape off as much of the green paste (chlorophyll) that's on the muslin as you can and discard the liquid. Put the chlorophyll in the fridge for later.

Be careful not to overcook the marrow as it will melt away to nothing.

To make the garlic sauce

• Bring a pot of water to the boil and quickly blanch the garlic. Refresh in a bowl of ice water, then repeat the process twice more to rid the garlic of any bitterness. Put the garlic in a pan with the whipping cream and simmer until it is very tender. Transfer the garlic and cream to a blender and blitz for at least 5 minutes. To finish the sauce, add salt to taste and a teaspoon of the green chorophyll paste. Mix until the sauce is deep green in colour.

To make the shallot and parsley salad

• Mix the parsley leaves, shallots and capers in a bowl. Toss with olive oil, lemon juice and salt and pepper to taste.

To cook the marrow bones and snails

• Preheat the oven to 200°C/Gas 6. Season the cut side of the bones with salt and pepper. Place them on baking tray and roast for 8–10 minutes until golden and bubbling.

• Meanwhile, warm the garlic sauce and set aside. Heat a medium-sized frying pan and fry the snails in butter until golden and crisp. Add the marjoram, chives and shallots, and season with salt and pepper. Sauté the girolles.

To serve

Place a piece of cooked marrow bone in the centre of each plate. Swirl garlic sauce around it, add some snails and girolles and top the marrow with shallot and parsley salad.

Stuffed courgette flowers

Courgette flowers stuffed with seasonal vegetables make a perfect summer starter. The flowers don't last long so if you grow them in your garden, pick them just before using so they are as fresh as possible.

8 courgette flowers, small courgettes attached
1 teaspoon olive oil
100ml chicken stock (see p.258)

Stuffing
60g red pepper
30g yellow pepper
30g onion, peeled
40g aubergine
100g tomato
1 garlic clove
1 sprig thyme

2 tablespoons olive oil
1 egg yolk
160g Crowdie cheese (or other cream cheese)
salt and pepper

Sauce
½ onion, finely chopped
1 garlic clove
1 tablespoon olive oil
100g tomato, chopped
10 basil leaves

Flower tempura
1 tablespoon flour
1 tablespoon plain flour
4 courgette flowers

Garnish
50g red pepper, diced
30g aubergine, diced
30g courgette, diced

To serve

Gently heat the stuffed flowers on an oiled tray in the oven at 170°C/Gas 3. Transfer to the serving plate. Heat the sauce with the diced pepper, aubergine, courgette and basil and pour around the stuffed flowers. Place a deep-fried courgette flower on top.

To make the stuffing

- Finely dice all the vegetables for the stuffing and add the chopped garlic and thyme. Sauté gently in olive oil until cooked. Mix together the egg yolk and cheese and add to the diced vegetables. Season to taste.

To prepare the courgette flowers

- Pull back the outer petals of the flowers and gently remove the stigma, making sure not to tear or separate any petals. Fill a piping bag with the stuffing mixture.

- Pipe the stuffing right into the centre of each flower and all the way up. Twist the tips of the flower to close. Heat the olive oil in a frying pan and gently fry the stuffed flowers. Add 20ml chicken stock, cover and cook for 10 minutes, adding more stock if needed.

To make the sauce

- Sweat the onion and garlic in olive oil. Add the tomato and the basil and cook for 30 minutes. Pass through a fine sieve and reduce until the sauce coats the back of a spoon. Dice the pepper, aubergine and courgette for the garnish.

To prepare the flower tempura

- Mix the flour and cornflour with ice-cold water until you have a smooth paste. Brush the tempura batter onto the courgette flowers for the garnish and deep fry, one at a time, in hot vegetable oil until crispy. Drain on kitchen paper.

If you don't have a piping bag, use a plastic
sandwich bag with the corner cut off.

Roast rib-eye
with wedge fries and béarnaise sauce

This dish is ideal for Sunday lunch and one we often cook. Take the steaks out of the fridge at least 30 minutes before you start cooking so the meat can come to room temperature.

4 rib-eye steaks, about
    300g each
2 teaspoons vegetable oil
salt and pepper

Wedge fries
4 potatoes, such as King
    Edward
2 tablespoons olive oil
pinch of paprika
1 sprig of thyme, chopped
salt and pepper

2 teaspoons chopped
    shallots
8–10 flat-leaf parsley leaves
1 teaspoon chopped
    chives

Béarnaise sauce
50ml white wine vinegar
5 peppercorns, crushed
1 shallot, peeled and finely
    sliced
5 sprigs of tarragon

2 egg yolks
150g clarified butter (p.264)
1 sprig chervil

Roast tomatoes
4 large vine-ripened
    tomatoes
1 tablespoon olive oil
2 sprigs of thyme
2 garlic cloves, peeled and
    thinly sliced
salt and pepper

To serve
Serve the steak with some wedge fries and a roast tomato, with the béarnaise sauce on the side.

To prepare the wedge fries
• Scrub the potatoes and cut each one lengthwise into 8 wedges. Toss the potatoes in a large bowl with the olive oil, paprika, thyme, salt and pepper. Place on a parchment-lined baking tray and roast at 200°C/Gas 6 until crispy and golden – about 30–40 minutes. Add the shallots near the end of the cooking time – if added too soon they will taste bitter. Remove from the oven and add the chopped parsley and chives.

To make the béarnaise sauce
• Place the vinegar, peppercorns, shallot and tarragon stalks in a pan (reserve the tarragon leaves for later). Reduce until you have only about 1 tablespoon of liquid. Add the egg yolks, then add a teaspoon of water and whisk over a very low heat until the egg yolks leave a trail in the bottom of the pan – this means they are cooked. Don't cook them too long or you will make scrambled eggs! Remove the pan from the heat and slowly add the clarified butter. Continue to whisk until all the butter has been added. Pass the sauce through a sieve and add the chopped tarragon leaves and chervil.

To roast the tomatoes
• Toss all ingredients in a bowl. Put in a roasting dish and roast in a hot oven (200°C/Gas 6) for 7–8 minutes or until tender.

To cook the steaks
• Heat a heavy-bottomed pan on the stove and sear the seasoned steaks in the vegetable oil until golden brown all over – about 3–4 minutes on each side. Put the pan with the steaks into the middle of the oven with the potatoes and cook for 2–3 minutes more, depending on how rare you want your meat. Remove the steaks from the pan and set aside to rest.

When searing steak, make sure the oil is smoking before adding the meat. If the oil is not hot enough, the steak will poach instead of sear.

Rump of lamb
with baby gem lettuce and lettuce sauce

In the restaurant I like to serve this rump of lamb with some sliced lamb belly and kidney, but you could make just the rump and lettuce sauce and it will still be delicious. However, the belly and the kidneys aren't difficult to prepare and the belly can be made the day before, then sliced and cooked when you're ready.

4 lamb rumps, about 250g
   each
2 baby gem lettuces
1 teaspoon vegetable oil
salt and pepper

Lamb belly
1 lamb belly
1 tablespoon ground cumin
1 tablespoon fennel seeds
salt and pepper
olive oil
vegetable oil

Lamb kidneys
2 lamb kidneys, cleaned
   and halved

Lettuce sauce
4 baby gem lettuce,
   roughly chopped
1 onion, thinly sliced
1 teaspoon vegetable oil
pinch of salt
250ml chicken stock
   (see p.258)
250ml whipping cream

A sign of a tasty rump of lamb is a good amount of fat on it.

To prepare the lamb belly

Season the lamb belly all over with cumin, fennel seeds, salt and pepper. Roll it up, tie with string to secure and place in a cast-iron casserole. Cover with olive oil – you'll need quite a lot. Cook gently in a slow oven, 170°C/Gas 3, for 4–5 hours until very tender. Remove the belly from the pot and allow to drain. Wrap it tightly in clingfilm and leave to set in the fridge at least 2 hours until solid. When you're ready to serve, cut the lamb belly into slices about 1.5cm thick. Fry with a teaspoon of vegetable oil for about 4 minutes each side until golden brown.

To make the lettuce sauce

Bring a large saucepan of water to the boil, add salt and quickly blanch the baby gem in the boiling water for 30 seconds. Carefully remove and immediately place in a bowl of iced water for 2 minutes. Squeeze out any excess moisture and set aside in fridge. (Blanching, and then chilling right away, helps to maintain a bright green colour.)

In the meantime, slowly sweat the onion in a heavy-bottomed pot with the vegetable oil and a pinch of salt. Once the onions are soft (with no colour) add the chicken stock and cream. Reduce by almost two-fifths and transfer to a blender. Add the chilled lettuce and blitz for 5 minutes or until smooth. Set aside.

To cook the lamb rumps

Preheat the oven to 200°C/Gas 6. Season the meat with salt and pepper and brown on all sides in a hot pan. Transfer to the hot oven for 4–6 minutes for medium-rare lamb. Let the meat rest for at least 10 minutes to retain its juices.

To cook the baby gems
- Cut the baby gems in half and remove any outer and damaged leaves. While the lamb is resting, season the lettuces and place them in a hot pan, cut side down, with a teaspoon of oil. Sear the lettuce until golden brown.

To cook the lamb kidneys
- Season the kidneys with salt and pepper and cook in a hot pan for 2–3 minutes until nice and pink.

To serve
Warm the lettuce sauce and spoon some onto each plate. Top with the rested, sliced rump. Garnish the plate with golden-brown baby gem lettuce, a slice of crispy lamb belly and half a kidney.

Boned and rolled pig's head
with langoustines and a crispy ear salad

Serves 4

This is my signature dish and one I'm particularly proud of.
It takes a lot of preparation and care but is well worth it.

1 pig's head, de-boned and tied	1 sprig of thyme	salt and pepper
2 carrots, roughly chopped	2 pig's ears	olive oil
1 celery stick, chopped	1 teaspoon herbes de Provence	12 langoustines
1 white onion, chopped	1 teaspoon ground cumin	sauce Gribiche (see p.263)
2 bay leaves	1 teaspoon fennel seeds	tomato concasse (see p.261)
		80g mixed salad leaves

Preparing the pig's head
- Start by removing all the hair with a blowtorch. Cut down the middle of the head, all the way to the snout, and then carefully cut away the flesh at each side of the head, keeping the meat attached to the skin. Tie with butcher's string. If you don't want to do this yourself, ask your butcher to bone and tie the head for you. Place the tied pig's head, carrots, celery, onion, bay leaves and thyme into a very large stock pot. Cover with about 2 litres of water, bring to the boil and cook for 1 hour.

- Remove all the hairs from the ears with a blowtorch and wrap them in muslin. Add the ears to the pot with the pig's head and cook for another 4 hours. Top up with boiling water as necessary to ensure the ears remain covered. At end of the cooking time, take the pot off the heat, remove the ears and set them aside, and leave the pig's head to cool.

116

To serve
On each plate, place a few salad leaves with a teaspoon of sauce Gribiche. Place a slice of the rolled pig's head on the salad and add the tomato concasse on top of this. Decorate with some crispy pig's ears and serve with the langoustines.

Rolling the pig's head

- Remove the cheeks from the pig's head and separate the fat and meat from the skin. Set the meat aside and discard the fat. Lay a piece of clingfilm on a chopping board and place the skin, outer side down, on the clingfilm.

- Shred the meat from the pig's cheeks and mix with the herbes de Provence, cumin, fennel seeds, a pinch of salt and some freshly ground pepper.

- Lay a line of the cheek meat mix in the middle of the skin and roll it into a sausage about 6cm in diameter. Wrap tightly in clingfilm and leave in the fridge to set for 12 hours. When you are ready to serve, cut the sausage into 3cm thick slices and fry them in olive oil until crispy on the outside and warm in the middle.

To make the crispy pig's ears

- Remove the cooked pig's ears from the muslin and trim off the muscles. Wrap the ears in clingfilm and put in the fridge under a heavy weight for 24 hours.

- Preheat the oven to 170°C/Gas 3. Shred the ears very finely with a sharp knife. Heat the olive oil in an ovenproof frying pan and add the shredded ears, spreading them evenly. Fry for a minute or two and then place the pan with the ears in the oven for 15–20 minutes until crispy. Keep warm until needed.

To cook the langoustines

- Peel the langoustines, leaving only the end tail in the shell, and remove the dark intestinal tracts. Heat a heavy-bottomed pan and add olive oil. Season the langoustines and pan-fry for 1–2 minutes depending on size.

117

Sea urchin soup

 Serves 6

I first cooked sea urchins when my lobster supplier suggested them to me – the urchins get caught in the lobster creels.

6 sea urchins
100g carrot, chopped
100g fennel, chopped

100g celery, chopped
1 teaspoon vegetable oil
100g samphire

150ml white wine sauce
  (see p.174)
1 lemon
rock salt for serving

Preparing the sea urchins

- Urchin spines are sharp so wear gloves or use a thick cloth when handling them. Using scissors with a pointy tip, cut off the top quarter of the shell, beginning from the soft area where there are no spines (the mouth). Discard the lid. Remove the digestive organ (middle of urchin). With a spoon, gently remove the coral (eggs) and set aside. Strain and reserve the liquid from inside the shells. Be very careful with the shells as you will need them for serving the soup.

Making the vegetable mix and the soup

- Sweat the carrot, fennel and celery in a pan with the oil until soft. Add the samphire and cook until warmed through. Set aside.

- Put the white wine sauce and the strained liquid from the urchins into a pan and warm over a low flame. Be careful not to over-heat. Add some of the urchin eggs, then blitz to the desired consistency. The eggs thicken the soup so add more as necessary. Finish with a squeeze of lemon.

To serve

Warm the empty shells in the oven. Take them out and place a large spoonful of the vegetable mix into each shell. Froth the soup with a hand whisk and ladle into the shells. Place a shell on each plate, using a bed of rock salt to keep the shell steady.

Mackerel tartare

½ cucumber, halved lengthwise and thinly sliced	½ tablespoon chopped shallots	½ cup beetroot purée (see p.260)
2 quails' eggs	1 teaspoon chopped chives	2 tablespoons crème fraîche
1 fresh mackerel	2 teaspoons soy sauce	salt and pepper
1 teaspoon olive oil	1 teaspoon rice vinegar	4 sprigs chervil (optional)

- Start by placing a small chopping board in the freezer. You will need this when chopping the mackerel later on.

- Take 4 round moulds, 8cm in diameter. Line the insides with overlapping pieces of cucumber. Set aside in the fridge. Cook the quails' eggs by putting them into boiling water for 2 minutes and 45 seconds. Remove and plunge into iced water before peeling.

- Fillet the mackerel and remove the skin. Cut the flesh from both sides of the bone to make 4 fillets. Take the chopping board out of the freezer and chop the mackerel into small neat dice. Put the diced fish into a bowl and place this into another bowl filled with ice.

- Add the olive oil, shallots, chives, soy and vinegar to the chopped mackerel and season with salt and pepper to taste. Leave for a few minutes so the flavours can infuse, then spoon into cucumber-lined moulds, filling them three-quarters full. Top with beetroot purée filling to the top of the cucumber slices.

To serve

Remove the mould once placed on the plate. Top with a spoonful of crème fraîche and add half an egg and a sprig of chervil.

Season the mackerel just before serving as the vinegar will start to cook it slowly if seasoned too far in advance.

Spiced aubergine
with Scottish smoked salmon

1 onion, diced
3 tablespoons olive oil
1 garlic clove, chopped
1 teaspoon curry powder
3 aubergines, cut into 1cm cubes
2 teaspoons cumin powder

2 teaspoons smoked paprika
2 spring onions, thinly sliced
4–6 basil leaves, cut into thin strips
smoked salmon

crème fraîche
1 lemon
melba toast, optional (see p.264)
15 sprigs chervil or dill
salt and pepper

- Sweat the diced onion in a heavy-bottomed frying pan with 1 tablespoon of the olive oil and the garlic, curry powder, salt and pepper. It's important to use a heavy pan so the onion cooks evenly without burning. Once the onion is soft, set it aside.

- Heat the frying pan and add the rest of the olive oil and the cubes of aubergine. Sprinkle with cumin powder and smoked paprika and cook until golden brown. It's best to do this in batches, taking care not to overcrowd the pan. If you put too much aubergine in at once it will steam instead of caramelise and lose its flavour. Aubergine soaks up oil so strain the cubes in a large sieve or colander after cooking to remove any excess oil. Mix the aubergine into the onions and cook gently for 8–10 minutes.

- When you're ready to serve, warm the aubergine and onion mixture and fold in the spring onions and basil leaves.

To serve
Place a few slices of smoked salmon on the plate. Add the aubergine mix and a spoonful of crème fraîche. Serve with lemon wedges and melba toast and sprinkle with chervil or dill.

Make sure you drain the aubergine as it acts like a sponge once fried.

Potatoes boulangère

The liquid used in this French classic can be varied according to what you are serving the dish with. Use lamb stock for serving with lamb, fish stock with fish and so on, to get the right combination of flavours on the plate.

1 teaspoon vegetable oil
1 onion, thinly sliced
1 leek, cut into thin strips
1 teaspoon herbes de Provence

1 garlic clove, minced
1 teaspoon fennel seeds
salt and pepper
butter

700g waxy potatoes such as Maris Piper, sliced as thinly as possible
500ml fish stock (see p.259)

- Heat the vegetable oil in a heavy-based pot and slowly sweat the onion until translucent. Add the leek, herbs, fennel seeds and garlic, then cook for another 5–10 minutes over low heat. Check for seasoning.

- Butter a suitable dish about 23cm in diameter. Arrange a layer of overlapping potato slices, then a layer of the onion and leek mix and season. Continue layering until the dish is full, finishing with a layer of potato.

- Preheat the oven to 170°C/Gas 3. Heat the fish stock (do not boil) and pour it slowly into the dish until it just covers the top of the potatoes. Dot with a couple knobs of butter. Place the dish, uncovered, on a tray in the oven and cook for 1½ hours or until the potatoes are very soft and the top is golden brown. This goes well with roast meat as well as fish.

Oven-roasted John Dory

Serves 4

Like many fish, John Dory works best cooked on the bone – fish cooked this way is always more moist than fillets. When John Dory is really fresh it has an amazing green colour.

1 John Dory (1–1.2kg), cleaned and trimmed
1 tomato, chopped
1 fennel, quartered
½ lemon, sliced

½ head of garlic, split into cloves
3 sprigs of thyme
3 star anise
120ml chicken stock (see p.258)

- Preheat the oven to 180°C/Gas 4. Season the John Dory and place it in a heavy-bottomed oven dish (Le Creuset is ideal). Arrange the vegetables, lemon and garlic around the fish, and add the herbs and star anise. Pour over the stock.

- Roast for 20–25 minutes, basting every 5–10 minutes. Once the fish is cooked, pass the cooking liquid through a fine sieve. Discard the pulp and serve the liquid as a sauce. Serve with boulangère potatoes (see opposite).

To check whether the fish is cooked, place a needle between the neck and the head at the thickest part and then gently bring it to your lip. If the needle is warm, the fish is ready!

123

Roasted monkfish
wrapped in pancetta

Serves 2

Monkfish is a meaty fish and goes well with pancetta. The flavours and fat of the pancetta are easily absorbed by the monkfish and give the flesh a moist flavour.

1 teaspoon chopped dill	1 tablespoon roughly	10–15 thin slices
1 teaspoon chopped flat-leaf parsley	chopped olives	unsmoked pancetta
zest of 1 lemon	1 monkfish tail, 400–450g	1 tablespoon vegetable oil
	salt and pepper	

- Mix the chopped herbs, lemon zest and olives. Season the monkfish with salt and pepper and then roll it in the herb mixture.

- Lay out the slices of pancetta, overlapping them slightly. Place the seasoned monkfish in the middle and fold the pancetta over the monkfish to cover it. Using butcher's string, tie round the fish at 2cm intervals to keep everything together while cooking. Chill in the fridge for 1 hour.

- Preheat the oven to 200°C/Gas 6. Heat the oil in a pan and brown the monkfish on all sides until golden. Transfer to the hot oven for 7–8 minutes to finish cooking. Let it rest for 3–4 minutes.

To serve

Remove the string and cut the monkfish into portions. Serve with a shellfish marinière (see p.132).

If you have a good relationship with your fishmonger, ask for monkfish cheeks – they are delicious.

Sautéed langoustines
in garlic butter

Few things taste better than freshly caught langoustines on a summer day. This recipe is one of the easiest to do, but also one of the tastiest. I keep it as simple as possible by adding only a touch of garlic and parsley to the fresh langoustines, as the herbs should enhance the dish and not overpower the flavour. This is served with some fresh bread and a crispy glass of dry Riesling, and is a favourite of mine.

8 langoustine tails
1 tablespoon olive oil
salt

50g unsalted butter
1 garlic clove, peeled and
    chopped

2 tablespoons chopped
    flat-leaf parsley
1 lemon

- Peel the langoustines and remove the dark intestinal tracts. Heat a heavy-bottomed pan and add the olive oil.

- Season the langoustine tails with salt and add them to the pan. Cook for 1½–2 minutes. Add the butter, garlic, parsley and a squeeze of lemon and serve.

To serve
Serve with some rustic bread to soak up the garlicky juices.

Kitchin lobster thermidor

This lobster dish can easily be prepared a few hours in advance and kept it in the fridge until guests arrive. Ten minutes before you sit down for your meal, all you need to do is put the dish in the oven. At the restaurant we use creel-caught lobsters which are native to the Scottish waters. Be aware that some fishmongers sell Canadian lobsters which don't have the flavour of those from the British Isles. Lobsters can be expensive so check that what you buy is fresh and good quality. Make sure that the lobsters are alive when you buy them from the fishmonger and don't ever be tempted to buy lobsters that are not moving, as they definitely will not be fresh.

2 lobsters, about 500g each
100ml white wine sauce (see p.174)
25g béchamel sauce (see p.261)

½ teaspoon English mustard
2 tablespoons cooked girolles (see p.105)
2 artichoke hearts, sliced (can be fresh or tinned)
salt

1 spring onion, thinly sliced
salt and pepper
2 sprigs tarragon, chopped
20g Parmesan cheese, grated

To serve
Sprinkle with some fresh herbs and serve straight away while hot.

To prepare the lobster
- Bring a large pan of water to the boil and add a handful of salt so the water tastes salty. Plunge the lobster into the boiling water for 1 minute. This kills it instantly and humanely. Remove the lobster from the pot and leave to cool for 2–3 minutes before proceeding.

- Cut the lobster in half, starting at the head and working towards the tail. Remove the claws and submerge them in boiling water for 5 minutes. Leave to cool and then remove all the meat from the claws. Remove all the meat from the halved body as well as the coral. Set aside.

To make the sauce
- Add the white wine sauce to the béchamel and whisk continuously over a low heat until the sauce thickens. Add the English mustard, girolles, artichoke hearts, spring onion and chopped tarragon.

Assembling the dish
- Add the lobster meat and claws to the sauce. Spoon the mixture back into lobster body and sprinkle with Parmesan. Place on a baking tray and put into a hot oven, 190°C/Gas 5, and cook for 8–10 minutes.

Always buy female lobsters if you can – the flesh is much sweeter.

Octopus carpaccio

Serves 4–6

The idea for this dish comes from my close friend Raphael Duntoye, who is a fantastic chef. I have taken the basis of his octopus dish and added my own twist. I serve the octopus with razor clams, scallops and langoustines, but it is delicious by itself.

2 carrots, chopped
2 onions, chopped
2 celery sticks, chopped
2 leeks, chopped
240ml soy sauce
4 star anise
1 large piece of fresh
ginger

10 cardamom pods,
crushed
2 whole octopus, cleaned
and previously frozen
Maldon sea salt
cracked black pepper
fresh herbs

Lemon caper dressing
1 lemon, zest and juice
1 tablespoon finely
chopped shallot
1 tablespoon capers
4 tablespoons olive oil
salt and pepper

To serve
Slice the octopus roll very thinly and arrange 5–6 rounds on each plate. Brush with lemon caper dressing and season with Maldon sea salt and cracked black pepper. Garnish with fresh herbs and some pickled vegetables if you like.

- In a large pan of water, bring the vegetables, soy and spices to the boil. Put the octopus into the pot, with enough water to submerge it, and bring back to the boil. Lower the heat and simmer for 40–60 minutes. The octopus is done when the thickest part, 'the shirt', where the head meets the tentacles, is easily pierced by a sharp knife. Take the pan off the heat and drain the octopus well.

- Remove the tentacles and discard the head. Lay out the tentacles on some clingfilm, alternating thickest to thinnest ends, and then roll up very tightly in the clingfilm. Pierce the finished roll with a sharp knife to let out any excess moisture. This allows the natural gelatin to set the roll that much better. Chill for 4–6 hours.

- Prepare the dressing by mixing all the ingredients together.

Freezing helps
to tenderise
fresh octopus.

Halibut
with salsa verde and citrus dressing

Serves 4

This citrus dressing works perfectly with the meatiness of the halibut and the sharpness of the salsa verde.

6–8 new potatoes
vegetable oil
100g fresh samphire
12 olives, pitted and chopped
300g baby spinach
2 large shallots, chopped
2 tablespoons chopped chives
4 x 200g halibut fillets
salt and pepper
chervil and dill

Salsa verde
2 tablespoons chopped basil
3 tablespoons chopped parsley
1 tablespoon chopped mint
3 tablespoons capers
4 anchovy fillets
1 garlic clove, peeled and chopped
1 tablespoon Dijon mustard
150ml olive oil
4 tablespoons sherry vinegar
1 lemon, zest and juice

Citrus dressing
4 lemons, segments and zest
8 cherry tomatoes, halved
1 teaspoon sugar
2 tablespoons olive oil

Croutons
2 slices white bread
1 teaspoon olive oil

Always use wild halibut as farmed halibut will have a slimy skin on it.

To prepare the salsa verde, dressing and croutons
- Blitz all the salsa ingredients together in a blender or food processor until smooth and set aside in the fridge.

- Toss the ingredients for the dressing together and set aside.

- For the croutons, cut the bread into small cubes. Heat the olive oil in a frying pan and fry the croutons until golden brown.

To prepare the potatoes
- Boil the potatoes in salted water until cooked. Cut the potatoes into slices 0.5cm thick. Fry these in a non-stick pan with a teaspoon of vegetable oil until crisp and golden brown. Add the samphire and chopped olives, then the baby spinach, shallots and chives.

To prepare the halibut
- Pat the fillets dry and season well with salt. Heat 2 tablespoons of vegetable oil in a non-stick pan over medium to high heat. Add the halibut fillets and cook until they are golden brown on both sides, turning once. This should take about 3 minutes each side. Allow the fish to rest for 3–4 minutes.

To serve
Spread some salsa verde onto each plate. Top with the vegetable mix and halibut. Spoon some citrus dressing over the halibut, add some croutons and and garnish with a few sprigs of chervil and dill.

Stuffed squid
with razor clams and pickled cucumber

Serves 2

I have used razor clams and baby squid for this recipe, but it works just as well with any other shellfish. The pickled cucumber and shellfish are a perfect match.

3 razor clams
50ml white wine
1 teaspoon chopped
   shallot
1 teaspoon chopped
   chives
1 tablespoon olive oil
100g fresh spinach
1 tablespoon chopped dill
salt and pepper
1 tablespoon chopped dill
2 baby squid, cleaned and
   tentacles removed

Pickled cucumber
125ml malt vinegar
240ml vegetable stock
   (or water)
500g sugar
1 bay leaf
4 sprigs of thyme
5 peppercorns
2 tablespoons salt
1 cucumber

Dressing
75ml pickling liquid
75ml olive oil
1 tablespoon finely
   chopped shallot
1 tablespoon chopped
   chives
1 tablespoon chopped
   tarragon
salt and pepper

To serve

Lay 3 or 4 strips of cucumber, slightly overlapping, on each plate and trim them neatly to fit the plate. Place a stuffed squid and a razor clam on top of the cucumber. Drizzle with dressing and garnish with freshly picked dill, chervil and celery leaves.

To prepare the pickled cucumber

• Place all the ingredients, except the cucumber, in a saucepan over a high heat. Bring to the boil, reduce the heat and simmer for 20 minutes. Strain and allow to cool.

• Thinly slice the unpeeled cucumber in long strips, cutting from tip to tip, preferably using a mandolin. Lay the slices flat in a long container and just cover with chilled pickling liquid. Set aside for at least 2 hours.

To make the dressing

• Mix all the ingredients together and season to taste.

To prepare the stuffed squid

• Wash the razor clams in cold water to remove any sand or grit. Heat a pan on top of the stove and add 1 razor clam and a splash of white wine. Cover and allow to steam for a minute or two until open. (A razor clam that doesn't open must be thrown away.) Add the chopped shallot and chives.

• Heat a tablespoon of olive oil in a pan, add the spinach and cook until wilted. Drain well, then place on some kitchen paper and squeeze out any excess water. Chop the spinach and razor clam together and add salt and pepper and chopped dill. Stuff the mixture into the baby squid and secure with a toothpick. Sear very quickly in a hot pan for 1– 2 minutes on each side.

• Cook the remaining razor clams as before.

The best way to keep razor clams is wrapped in
wet newspaper in the fridge.

Shellfish marinière

Be sure to wash all the shellfish well under cold running water to get rid of any sand before cooking them, and carefully pull the 'beards' off the mussels.

2 large shallots, peeled and thinly sliced	1 sprig of thyme	300ml white wine
1 tablespoon olive oil	400g mussels, washed and debearded	1 handful of flat-leaf parsley, roughly chopped
1 garlic clove, peeled and finely chopped	400g cockles, washed and cleaned	salt and pepper
1 bay leaf	400g razor clams, washed and cleaned	

To serve

Serve in deep bowls with some crusty bread on the side to mop up the juices.

- In a deep, heavy-bottomed saucepan, sauté the shallots in olive oil until soft and translucent. Season to taste. Add the garlic, bay leaf and thyme.

- Over a high heat, add the shellfish to the shallot mixture and toss to coat. Pour in the wine and cover with a lid. Cook for 5–7 minutes until the shellfish begin to open – discard any that do not open.

- Remove from the heat and mix in the fresh chopped parsley.

Use a shell to scoop out the flesh from the mussels instead of a knife and fork.

Scallops carpaccio

It's best to buy scallops in their shells and they are not hard to prepare. To open, carefully slip a thin, sharp knife between the two shells and cut through the large white muscle (abductor muscle) to release one side of the shell. Pry open the scallop and scoop out the contents. Separate the white meat and save the roes (coral) and outer skirts for sauces – they freeze very well, so you can keep them in a bag in the freezer until needed.

4 large hand-dived scallops	zest and juice of 1 lemon	4 radishes
50ml olive oil	1 teaspoon poppy seeds	1 Granny Smith apple
2 shallots, peeled and finely chopped	sea salt and cracked black pepper	small handful of red amaranth leaves

To serve

Cut the radishes and apple into strips and slices. Add a squeeze of lemon juice and arrange the apple and radishes over the scallops. At the very last minute, add the red amaranth as a garnish.

- Open the scallops and slice them thinly onto a plate. This can be done ahead of time, but everything else for this dish should be prepared and cut at the last minute for maximum flavour.

- Brush the scallop slices with olive oil and sprinkle with shallots, lemon zest and poppy seeds. Season with sea salt and cracked black pepper.

Scallops
with sauce vierge

This light sauce goes well with all freshly caught fish. Use a medium-strength olive oil which goes well with the citrus.

4 large scallops in their shells
1 teaspoon vegetable oil
10 sprigs each chervil and dill
salt and pepper

Sauce vierge
40ml olive oil
1 garlic clove, peeled and finely chopped
juice of 1 lemon
1 teaspoon very finely sliced preserved lemon rind (see p.264)

2 tomatoes, peeled, seeded and chopped
5 basil leaves, sliced finely
1 teaspoon finely chopped chives
salt and pepper

To make the sauce
- Warm the olive oil slightly in a pan over medium heat. Remove from the heat and add the garlic, lemon juice, preserved lemon rind, tomatoes, basil and chives. Season to taste and set aside so the flavours can infuse while you cook the scallops.

To prepare the scallops
- Open the scallops as described opposite, keeping four of the shells. Rinse the white meat, and keep in the fridge on paper towels until needed. Rinse the shells and pat dry.

- To cook the scallops, heat the vegetable oil in a large, non-stick pan over a high heat. Cut each scallop in half, season and sear them in the oil until golden brown on both sides. Take care not to over cook the scallops or they turn to rubber.

To serve
Place two pieces of scallop into each shell and spoon over some sauce. Garnish with picked chervil and dill leaves.

Summer berries

with cottage cheese cream and almond tuiles

This dish looks great and is simple to make as everything can be prepared in advance. Use any combination of summer berries.

	Cottage cheese cream	Almond tuiles
100g redcurrants	200ml whipping cream	200g icing sugar
100g blueberries	200g cottage cheese	50g flour
100g blackberries	1 lime, zest and juice	70g flaked almonds
100g strawberries		juice and zest of 1 orange
100g raspberries		70g butter, melted
fresh mint leaves		
icing sugar		

To make the cottage cheese cream

- Whip the cream to firm peaks. Fold in the cottage cheese, lime zest and juice and mix together. Leave in the fridge until ready to serve.

To make the almond tuiles

- Make the tuiles a day or two ahead so they can set. Preheat the oven to 200°C/Gas 6. Sift the icing sugar and flour together and mix with the flaked almonds, juice and zest, and the melted butter. Line a large baking sheet with parchment. Drop rounded teaspoons of the mixture onto the baking sheet and spread them out with the back of a spoon to make circles about 5cm in diameter – wet the spoon with water to prevent it sticking. Leave some space between each tuile as they will expand. You need to make 16 altogether.

- Bake the biscuits for 6–8 minutes until nicely golden. Time them carefully, as if overcooked the tuile will be bitter and brittle, and if undercooked they are too soft and pliable. While they are still warm, trim the discs to the desired shape. Leave them to rest and cool.

To assemble the dish

To serve

Place a few fruits on top as a garnish and add some fresh mint and icing sugar. Serve immediately.

- Wash the berries well. Hull the strawberries and cut them in half if they are large. Spoon a small amount of cottage cheese cream onto each plate. Top that with a tuile biscuit and begin to make layers by arranging a selection of berries on the inside edge of the tuile leaving room in the middle for more cream. Top with tuile and repeat. Finish with a tuile on top and place a teaspoon of cream in the middle of the tuile.

Summer pudding
with fruit coulis

Serves 6

This classic British dessert is made of sliced white bread layered in a deep bowl with stewed or macerated berries. Blueberries, raspberries, strawberries and brambles all work well. In my version I have replaced the bread with jaconde biscuits as I think this adds great texture to the dish.

350g assorted summer
   berries
mint, thinly sliced for
   garnish

Fruit coulis
200g berries
50g sugar

Jaconde biscuits
3 eggs
20g honey
95g sugar
3 egg whites
30g flour
125g ground almonds
25g butter, melted

To serve
Carefully turn out each pudding onto the centre of each plate. Add fresh berries for decoration and some mint leaves.

To make the fruit coulis
- Simmer the berries for the coulis in a pan with 4 tablespoons of water and the sugar until they have softened. Blend and then pass through a fine sieve.

To make the jaconde biscuits
- Preheat the oven to 180–200°C/Gas 5–6. Line a baking sheet with parchment. Whisk the eggs, honey and 70g of the sugar together until pale and increased in volume. Whisk the egg whites until they form soft peaks. Gradually add the rest of the sugar and continue whisking until stiff. Fold the egg whites into the egg and honey mixture, then gently fold in the flour, ground almonds and melted butter.

- Spread the mixture evenly over the baking tray. Bake in the preheated oven until golden, about 10 minutes. Leave to cool and then cut into shapes to fit your pudding moulds.

Assembling the pudding
- You will need some individual pudding moulds. Place a jaconde biscuit in the bottom of each mould and some neatly around the sides. Top with berries and pour some fruit coulis on top. Repeat until the mould is almost full and top with jaconde biscuit and more coulis. Press the top down firmly and leave the puddings to set in the fridge.

Add a splash of your favourite liqueur when making the fruit coulis.

Hibiscus pannacotta
with floating islands and strawberries

This is a great combination, but the pannacotta is also delicious on its own with strawberries or ice cream.

Hibiscus pannacotta
400ml whipping cream
100ml milk
70g sugar
15g dried hibiscus flowers
1½ leaves gelatin

Floating islands
1 egg white
1 tablespoon caster sugar
zest of ½ lemon
350ml milk (for poaching)

Hibiscus syrup
1 tablespoon dried hibiscus
  flowers
100g caster sugar

Garnish
6 strawberries per serving
sprigs of lemon thyme
tuile biscuits (see p.265)

To serve

Unmould the pannacotta and place it in the centre of the plate. Place a floating island on top of the pannacotta and add fresh strawberries and hibiscus syrup. Garnish with a sprig of lemon thyme and a crispy tuile.

To make the hibiscus pannacotta

Mix together the cream, milk, sugar and hibiscus flowers. Heat over a medium flame until just boiling. Take off the heat and leave to infuse for 15 minutes. Soak the gelatin in cold water for 3–4 minutes until soft, then squeeze out the excess moisture. Mix the gelatin into the hibiscus/cream mix while it is still hot and pass through a sieve. Keep the liquid and discard the flowers.

Take 8 individual non-stick ramekins or one large non-stick mould. If you don't have non-stick dishes, grease them lightly. Pour in the pannacotta mixture and leave to set in the fridge until firm, about 1–2 hours.

Hibiscus syrup

Boil the hibiscus flowers and sugar with 200ml of water until the mixture thickens and just coats the back of a spoon. Leave it to cool – it will thicken further.

Floating islands

Whisk the egg white until it forms soft peaks. Add the sugar and whisk until stiff. Fold in the lemon zest.

Heat the milk in a small pan. Drop tablespoons of egg white into the hot milk, turning to coat, and cook them gently for 1–2 minutes. You will need 8 islands. Gently remove the islands with a slotted spoon, drain and set aside until you are ready to serve.

The unique flavour of the hibiscus is fantastic with summer fruits. Buy dried hibiscus flowers from spice shops or on the internet.

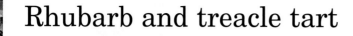

Rhubarb and treacle tart

Serves 6–8

The acidity of the rhubarb is a perfect match to the sweetness of the treacle in this tart. An ideal Sunday lunch dessert, this is fantastic with clotted cream, ice cream or custard. I warn you – it will disappear fast!

To serve

Dust with icing sugar and cut into portions. Serve with cream, ice cream or custard (see p.265).

Sweet pastry	Rhubarb	Treacle mix
250g plain flour	3 sticks of rhubarb, cut into 10cm pieces	125g soft butter
50g icing sugar	285g sugar	50g sugar
175g unsalted butter	zest of 1 lemon	2 large eggs
1 egg		150g golden syrup
1 egg yolk	extra icing sugar for dusting the tart	20g flour
		125g ground almonds

To make the pastry

- Sift the flour and sugar together. Pulse with the butter in a food processor until the mixture resembles breadcrumbs. Mix in the egg and knead gently until the dough clings together. Flatten to a round, wrap in clingfilm and chill for 30 minutes.

- Preheat the oven to 200°C/Gas 6. Roll out the pastry to a thickness of 4mm and line a 23cm pie tin or fluted flan tin. Trim the edges, cover the pastry with parchment paper and pour in 3 cups of baking beans. Bake for 10 minutes, then remove the beans and paper and cook for another 10–12 minutes or until golden. While the pastry is still warm, brush the inside with egg yolk. This helps to seal the pastry from the tart filling so the base stays crispy.

To prepare the rhubarb

- Toss the pieces of rhubarb with the sugar and zest. Put in a deep ovenproof dish and cover with foil. Bake at 180°C/Gas 5 for 45–60 minutes until the rhubarb is very tender and the sugar is completely dissolved. Strain the rhubarb, reserving the juice, and set aside. Reduce the cooking liquid until it is thick enough to coat the back of a spoon. Set aside to use later as a glaze.

To prepare the treacle mix

- Beat the butter with the sugar until light and fluffy. Beat in the eggs one at a time, then fold in the golden syrup followed by the flour and ground almonds.

To assemble the tart

- Preheat the oven to 180°C/Gas 5. Smooth the cooled rhubarb mix over the cooked pastry base. Pour in the treacle mix, covering the rhubarb evenly.

- Place on a baking tray and cook in the preheated oven for about 45 minutes or until golden brown. Leave to rest and cool for 25 minutes, then brush with the reduced rhubarb glaze.

Blackcurrant soufflé
with honeycomb ice cream

This soufflé is a delicate French dessert which needs careful preparation. Best made with locally grown blackcurrants.

Soufflé
50g butter
50g dark chocolate, grated
200g blackcurrant purée
45g caster sugar
2 egg yolks

1 egg
1 tablespoon flour
7 egg whites
75g sugar
icing sugar for dusting

Honeycomb ice cream
5 egg yolks
130g heather honey
250ml milk
250ml whipping cream
150g honeycomb

To make the honeycomb ice cream

- Using a whisk, beat the egg yolks and honey in a bowl until pale and slightly thickened. Meanwhile, heat the milk and cream to simmering point and set aside. In a heavy-bottomed pot, warm the beaten eggs and honey over very low heat, stirring constantly. Gradually stir in the hot milk and cream. Cook over low heat stirring with a wooden spoon until the mix thickens just enough to coat the back of the spoon. Take off the heat.

- Strain the custard in a large bowl set over iced water. Pour into an ice cream machine and begin to churn. Roughly chop the honeycomb and add it to the ice cream. Churn until just frozen, place into a airtight plastic container and freeze for at least 3 hours before use.

Preparing the moulds

- Take 4 coffee-cup size soufflé dishes (or ramekin dishes) and brush generously with softened butter. Tip grated chocolate into each dish, rolling it around and making sure the inside is completely covered. Leave it to chill in the fridge.

To serve
Dust the soufflés with icing sugar. Serve the ice cream on the side or, at the table, make a small dip in each soufflé with a spoon and add a generous scoop of honeycomb ice cream.

For the soufflé base

- In a heavy pan, bring the blackcurrant purée and sugar to the boil. Stir in the egg yolks, egg and flour and bring the mixture back to boil, stirring constantly until thickened. Remove the pan from the heat and cover with clingfilm to prevent a skin forming. Allow to cool.

To make the soufflé

- Preheat the oven to 190°C/Gas 5. Put the soufflé base mixture, which should weigh about 350g, into a pan and warm it gently over a low heat. Meanwhile whisk the egg whites to firm peaks, then add the sugar and whisk until stiff. Fold the stiff whites and warmed soufflé base together and spoon the mixture into the prepared moulds. Pull a palette knife across the top of each dish to make it perfectly flat. Also run the end of your thumb around the inside edge of each dish as this helps the soufflés to rise evenly and prevents them sticking to the dish.

- Place the soufflés on a baking tray and cook in the preheated oven for 8 10 minutes until they have risen two-thirds in height. Don't open the oven while baking or the soufflés will collapse!

Honey parfait
with pickled plums and oat crumble

My favourite honey comes from Perthshire. The heather on the surrounding hills gives the honey a unique flavour.

Honey parfait
90g clear honey
4 egg yolks
300ml whipped cream
1 teaspoon Drambuie

Crumble mix
50g oats
50g pecans
1 teaspoon egg white
1 tablespoon icing sugar

Pickled plums
300ml red wine
1 tablespoon honey
3 teaspoons sugar
75ml white wine vinegar
2 cinnamon sticks
3 cloves
juice of ½ lemon
6 plums, thinly sliced

Plum crisps
1 plum
50g icing sugar

Garnish
1 plum, diced
fresh mint leaves

To serve
Arrange a circle of pickled plum slices on the plate. Unmould the parfait onto the plums and top with diced plums and oat crumble. Garnish with mint leaves and plum crisps.

To make the honey parfait
Heat the honey in a small pan, bring to the boil and set aside. In a small bowl, whisk the egg yolks until pale and thick. Slowly add the honey to the yolks, whisking until everything is combined. Whisk the cream to firm peaks and fold in the Drambuie. Fold the honey and egg yolk mixture into the whipped cream and Drambuie. Pour into moulds, about 7.5cm across and 5cm deep is a good size, and put in the freezer to set.

To make the plum crisps
Slice the plum thinly and place the slices on a baking tray lined with baking parchment. Dust generously with icing sugar, then turn the slices over and dust the other side. Dry in a cool oven (100°C/Gas ½) for about 2 hours, then check. If they are not yet crisp, cook for a while longer, but keep checking.

To make the crumble mix
Toss all the ingredients together and spread out on a baking tray lined with parchment. Bake at 180°C/Gas 4 for 6–8 minutes until golden brown.

To prepare the pickled plums
Place the red wine, honey, sugar, vinegar, cinnamon, cloves and lemon juice in a non-reactive pan (stainless steel or ceramic). Bring to the boil, then take off the heat and leave to infuse for 15 minutes. Strain and leave to cool. Once the pickling liquid has cooled to room temperature, slice the plums into thin discs and steep them in the liquid for at least 1 hour.

The parfait keeps for a few days in the freezer, so can be prepared in advance.

Gratin of red fruits
in white wine sabayon

This is a classic recipe and one that has been treasured for generations. Don't be afraid of using berries or fruits other than those I have suggested, as most combinations work well, but always remember to add some extra sugar if the berries are slightly sour in order to get that sweet taste. Fresh berries are best, but frozen are a great option too.

500g fresh berries

Fruit coulis
500g strawberries, raspberries, blackberries (fresh or frozen)
100g caster sugar
juice of 1 lemon

White wine sabayon
4 egg yolks
50g caster sugar
200ml white wine

To make the fruit coulis
- Place the berries in a large pot with 100ml of water. Stir in the sugar and cook over low heat to soften the fruit. Let the fruit cool slightly and then blitz in a blender until smooth. Strain the mixture through a sieve and stir in the lemon juice. Keep in fridge or freeze for later use.

To serve
Serve straight away with a dollop of vanilla ice cream if you wish.

To make the white wine sabayon
- Bring a pan of water to a gentle simmer. In a large bowl, whisk the egg yolks and sugar until slightly thickened and pale. Slowly add the wine. Place the bowl over the simmering water and whisk vigorously in a figure-of-eight motion for 6–8 minutes until the mixture has increased in volume – be careful not to let it get too hot or the eggs will scramble. Take off the heat and whisk with an electric beater until the sauce is cool to touch.

To assemble the dish
- Preheat the grill. Warm the fresh berries in the fruit coulis and arrange in heatproof bowls. Pour the sabayon on top and place under a warm grill for 2–3 minutes until the sabayon is golden.

The sabayon is cooked when it leaves
a trail at the bottom of the pan.

Grouse

The glorious twelfth – the 12th August when the first grouse arrive to Scotland – is one of the most exciting moments in my kitchen year. I always like to make sure I get my hands on the very first grouse in the country.

In the afternoon of the 12th, I leave my kitchen straight after lunch service is finished and drive up to my gamekeeper in Dalkeith, about 45 minutes from Edinburgh, to collect my birds. The birds have been shot that same morning and are still warm when I collect them. It's vital for me to be able to serve grouse to my dinner guests the very first night they are available and very thrilling. I also know that some of my diners on that night will have travelled far afield to my restaurant in order to taste the first grouse. I don't want to disappoint them.

Thanks to my trusted gamekeeper Ronnie, I managed to get 30 newly shot birds on the very first day they were available this year. I was over the moon. With my grouse, I went straight back to The Kitchin, arriving just after 5pm to start the whole team plucking and preparing the beautiful birds. I can admit that my heart was pounding with excitement while preparing the grouse. It was one of those moments that has stayed in my mind – it was the middle of Edinburgh festival madness, the restaurant was full and all I could think about was getting the grouse and everything else ready. I love that sort of buzz and often find myself working best under severe pressure. The thought of providing my guests with the first grouse on the first day they're available in this country is just such a great satisfaction in itself. We sold 19 grouse that night! I couldn't have been happier.

I always only use young grouse, as I find them tender and tastier than the ones that have hung for a long time, but that is up to everyone's individual preferences. The unique flavour of the grouse is largely due to the fact that they live off the blueberries and heather from the Scottish hills. As I remove the stomach sack of the bird I usually find large amounts of heather from the hills wrapped up inside the young grouse – the bird's last meal – so I like to think that the grouse is seasoned by Nature itself.

Scottish grouse

Serves 2

2 grouse, prepared and
 wrapped in bacon
vegetable oil
50g celeriac, carrots, and
 celery, chopped into
 1cm dice
baby onions
2 sprigs of fresh thyme
1 tablespoon brandy
salt and pepper
250ml chicken stock
 (see p.258)

Bread sauce
250ml milk
½ large onion, peeled
2 cloves
1 tablespoon butter
110g white bread, crusts
 removed and cut into
 2cm cubes
salt
white pepper
1 teaspoon nutmeg

Game chips
1 large potato
300ml vegetable oil
salt

To serve

Serve the rested grouse
whole with pan juices,
vegetables, bread sauce,
game chips and some
sautéed spinach and
girolles (see p.105).
If you don't like bread
sauce, serve with some
celeriac purée (see p.260).

To prepare the grouse

Take the grouse out of the fridge so that they can come to room temperature before you start cooking. Preheat the oven to 200°C/Gas 6.

Heat a tablespoon of vegetable oil in a large heavy-bottomed roasting tin. Season the grouse very well, inside and out, then sear them in the pan until golden brown all over. Add the diced vegetables, baby onions and thyme sprigs to the pan. Place the grouse on one breast and roast in the hot oven for 3–4 minutes. Flip the birds onto the other breast and roast for another 3 minutes. Next pour brandy into both birds and place them on their back to finish roasting – another 5 minutes.

Remove the pan from the oven and leave the grouse to rest for 10 minutes breast upwards so the juices are evenly distributed. Keep all the pan juices and vegetables.

Put the roasting tin back on the heat on top of the stove and begin to reduce the cooking juices. Add the chicken stock, bring to the boil and let the sauce reduce and thicken. Take off the heat and pass through a fine sieve. Keep warm until ready to serve.

To make the bread sauce

Simmer the milk with the onion stuck with cloves and cook until the onion is tender. Strain the milk into a clean pan and add the butter. Next, whisk in the bread off the heat and mix until smooth. For a smoother sauce, use a hand blender. To finish, season with salt, white pepper and nutmeg.

To make the game chips

Using the criss-cross part of a mandolin, cut the potato into slices roughly 3mm thick. Warm the oil gently on the stove. Dip a slice into the oil to check the oil is hot enough to fry. Fry the potatoes until crispy. Drain on paper towel and season lightly with salt.

To check that the grouse is young, squeeze the top of the skull. If it's soft, it is a young bird.

Autumn

Autumn to me means the arrival of many delicious things in my kitchen.
One distinctive smell that captures autumn like nothing else is the smell of
chestnuts cooking. This takes me back to my years working as a young chef in
Paris and London, when I would often buy a warm bag of roasted chestnuts from
a street stall. I love the burnt, sweet, almost charcoaly aroma and always associate
it with autumn. I use chestnuts in my cooking to add texture and sweetness to
game dishes, especially venison, and I also adore chestnuts in desserts – with
autumn pears, for example.

I am passionate about game and always like to make sure I have as much game
on my menu as possible. I even compile a special celebration-of-game menu to
accompany the autumn à la carte dishes at the restaurant. The game season is
hugely exciting for me and I love the whole process – from receiving the animals
in their feathers or furs, plucking and preparing, and eventually serving them in the
restaurant. My kitchen is always at its busiest during the height of the game
season – and so is my mind, as I come up with exciting new dishes and methods
of cooking game. In my kitchen everyone is involved in every step of the game
process, which means that on a busy day in October some of my chefs will be
plucking or tying birds most of the day.

I spend a lot of time explaining the different methods of handling game to my
chefs, as I believe it is vital to learn the proper preparation techniques in order to
get the best from your ingredients. Cooking game is all about knowing your
produce and perfecting your skills so nothing goes to waste. One of the beauties
of game is the number of variations and dishes that can be made from the various
cuts. I use every part of the animal – from the prime loins of hare and venison for
roasting to the legs for braising or a ravioli dish. The carcasses are used to make
a delicious consommé.

Autumn

Ronnie Grigor, my gamekeeper, is a man of much wisdom. Based in the village of Humbie, outside Edinburgh, Ronnie, like many gamekeepers, carries on the traditions and knowledge of his father, grandfather and many generations before them. Ronnie knows his game, and for him and many others in his position it's not just a job – his life revolves around his work. He knows so much about the animals and their behaviour and I love to listen to his stories and his thoughts on upcoming shoots and the produce available. People like Ronnie are invaluable to me as a chef and a true inspiration.

In many kitchens, it has become a thing of the past to pluck and tie game birds but I feel it is important to keep these traditions going. I know that many British chefs today have never been taught the art of butchering and so feel uncomfortable doing all the work themselves. I appreciate that the process can

be time-consuming, but it is incredibly rewarding to follow the whole procedure through from start to finish – from Nature to Plate indeed! My autumn menu includes glorious grouse of course, but I also serve pheasant, venison, partridge, mallard and other delights. There is also a wonderful range of root vegetables in autumn, which accompany game dishes beautifully. I enjoy cooking celeriac, parsnip and turnip because of their unique flavours and I use them frequently throughout the autumn and winter months. I enjoy the adaptability of autumn vegetables and the many options they give me in my cooking – they are ideal for soups, purées, crisps and vegetable gratins and taste delicious simply roasted. Pumpkin is at its best in autumn and deserves our attention – it's not just for carving Halloween lanterns. Chopped, sautéed pumpkin is wonderful in vegetable gratins, and I use pumpkin to make delicious purées. I also

Autumn

make desserts based on pumpkin, because of its sweet flavour. Pumpkin and most other root vegetables go incredibly well together. Take butternut squash, celeriac, carrots, parsnips – whatever you have in your fridge from your autumn vegetable shopping – and create an outstanding hot soup. It's simple to make and just right on a cool autumn day.

British apples and other orchard fruits such as pears, plums and quince are at their best in autumn and have a sweet and fresh flavour. I always make jams and cordials as well as using fruit in my cooking. Don't be afraid of adding fruit to your vegetables or to your game dishes, it usually works wonders and adds new dimensions to dishes. I like using thinly sliced apples, poached plums or pan-fried pears with game to lighten the dish and add a touch of sweetness and extra flavour.

Beetroot is another autumn vegetable that I use a great deal as I love the flavour and colour. It contains key beneficial nutrients such as nitrate, which can also be found in leafy, green vegetables, and UK research suggests that beetroot juice can reduce blood pressure. I believe that beetroot in any shape or form is generally good for you. I often served my wife beetroot dishes while she was pregnant with our son and minutes after Kasper was born, weighing in at ten pounds, the midwife jokingly said, 'What did you feed her?' I answered, 'Beetroot!'

It was with great excitement that I recently discovered a new wild berry – sea buckthorn, also known as sea berry. The orange berries grow in abundance on the coasts of Scotland and I have now discovered some good places to pick them. Their prime time in Scotland is from September to February and they are said to have super-high vitamin components and are long believed to have health benefits. They are slightly tricky to pick, as they easily burst between your fingers, but I absolutely love their unique flavour – a sweet, honey-like taste, with a hint of citrus and exotic fruit. I like to use the berries in a refreshing sorbet and also serve them at The Kitchin with chocolate – a truly beautiful combination. Other under-used wild autumn berries that I use in my cooking are hawthorn and rosehips for their unusual flavours and interesting taste sensations.

Another autumn treat is fungi foraging. In Scotland in autumn I always make sure I go mushroom picking. But one of my most memorable experiences of fungi foraging was the time when I went truffle hunting in Alba in Italy – a region that is world famous for truffles. I was asked to buy some truffles for Sir Anthony Bamford's 60th birthday party when I was working for the family, and through my head chef in Monaco I got in touch with an Italian truffle master. We had an appointment to meet, but only after he had checked all my references and I had assured him I was honest and trustworthy and wanted to spend money. Not my own money I should add, but the money I was given by my employer to get him the very best truffles there were. The truffle master invited me for dinner with his wife. After several bottles of wine and long chats he must have thought I was decent enough and he agreed to pick me up the following day.

I was expecting the man to come and collect me with his dog, but instead he showed up in his 4x4 Porsche at my hotel and took me to a secret spot.

I got my truffles and the whole experience was something I will never forget.

But the story didn't end there. When I got back to the yacht where I was working at the time, anchored in Antibes on the French Riviera, I was told that Lady Bamford and Sir Anthony already had left for London and they needed the truffles for their party the next day. The Bamfords had taken their private jet, but I had no other option but to catch the next flight back to London on Easyjet. I packed up the truffles in plenty of rags and papers, placed them in a cool box and took this as my hand luggage. God knows how I managed to get through customs without suspicion. I placed the box in the overhead locker in the plane and as we landed, took it down and was met by the

distinctive pungent smell. A few people looked up, probably thinking I had a bad BO, but one guy leaned over and said, 'You've been to Alba, haven't you?'

The key to autumn cooking is to observe the produce around you. By experimenting with seasonal combinations you will find that many ingredients are naturally in tune. Let the colours of nature and the textures and flavours of autumn produce inspire you to be more adventurous in your cooking.

Autumn soups

Making delicious soups in autumn is quick and easy as there are so many wonderful ingredients. These are four of my personal favourites. By concentrating on the unique flavour of different ingredients I let the produce speak for itself. Each soup is not only incredibly tasty, but also a true delight to the eye because of the outstanding natural colours.

Jerusalem artichoke soup

Serves 4–6

10–12 Jerusalem artichokes
1 lemon
1 large onion, peeled and chopped
2 tablespoons vegetable oil
750ml chicken stock (see p.258)
150ml whipping cream
salt and pepper
croutons (see p.129)

- First, peel the artichokes with a vegetable peeler and place them in a bowl of cold water until needed. Add a squeeze of lemon juice to stop them going brown.

- In a large pan, sweat the chopped onion in the oil and add a pinch of salt. Cook for 5–6 minutes until soft. Meanwhile, dice the artichokes into rough 2cm cubes. Add them to the onions and sweat for a further 3–4 minutes. Pour in the chicken stock and cream to cover the artichokes and cook over a medium heat until the vegetables are soft. Add the juice of half the lemon and cook for 5 more minutes.

- Blitz the soup in a blender until smooth. If it is too thick, add a little more stock. Check the seasoning.

To serve
- Warm the soup through and serve with crispy croutons if you wish.

Beetroot soup

Serves 4–6

2 tablespoons vegetable oil
1 onion, peeled and sliced
5 large beetroot, peeled and sliced
1–2 teaspoons sherry vinegar
800ml chicken stock (see p.258)
150ml natural yoghurt
salt and pepper
10 chives, finely chopped

- Warm the oil in a large heavy-bottomed pan. Add the sliced onion, season well and cook over a low heat until very tender. Add the beetroot and the sherry vinegar and sweat for 10–15 minutes over medium heat.

- Meanwhile bring the chicken stock to the boil. Add the stock to the onions and beetroot and cook slowly until the beetroot is very soft. Add extra stock if the soup is too thick for your liking.

- Pour the soup into a blender and blitz until it is smooth and velvety. Add 90ml of the yoghurt to the soup and whisk well, reserving the rest to use as a garnish.

To serve
- Pour the soup into bowls and garnish with the rest of the yoghurt and the chopped chives.

Carrot and star anise soup

Serves 4–6

2 tablespoons vegetable oil
1 onion, peeled and sliced
2–3 whole star anise
10 carrots, peeled and sliced

750ml chicken stock (see p.258)
150ml whipping cream
salt and pepper
6 sprigs of chervil

- Heat the vegetable oil in a large heavy-bottomed pan and cook the onion over a medium heat until very soft. Add the star anise and some salt, then sweat gently for 3–4 minutes.

- Add the carrots to the onion and sweat gently for 2–3 minutes. Add the chicken stock and cream to the pan and cook for another 15–20 minutes until the carrots are soft.

- Remove the star anise and blitz the soup in a blender until it is smooth and silky. Check the seasoning.

To serve
- Pour the soup into bowls and garnish with sprigs of chervil.

Game consommé

Serves 4–6

1kg game carcasses such as pheasant, partridge, grouse, woodcock (ask your butcher)
2 tablespoons olive oil
2 carrots, peeled and chopped
2 celery sticks, chopped
1 large onion, quartered

1 bouquet garni
200g game trimmings
4 egg whites
salt and pepper

Garnish
a few diced root vegetables (optional)

To make the stock
- Preheat the oven to 200°C/Gas 6. Roast the game carcasses with the oil until golden – about 30 minutes. Put the carcasses in a large pan with 2–3 litres of cold water. Over a medium heat, bring the water to simmering point, removing any scum that floats to the top with a ladle. Add the vegetables and bouquet garni and leave to simmer for 1½ hours. Strain the stock, cool and refrigerate.

To clarify the stock
- Put the game trimmings into a food processor with the egg whites and blitz until a fine paste is formed. Remove any fat from the top of the stock and pour the stock into a pan. Add the paste and mix well with a wooden spoon. Put the pan on the stove and heat, stirring constantly so the paste doesn't catch at the bottom of the pan.

- When the stock reaches 60–70°C a crust will start to form. Lower the heat, stop stirring and leave the consommé to cook over a medium heat for 30 minutes. At the end of this time, a thick, fatty crust will have developed on top, leaving a clear consommé underneath.

To serve
- Blanch the root vegetables in boiling water if using. Carefully remove a bit of the crust and scoop out the consommé with a ladle. Pass it through a sieve lined with a fine muslin cloth and check the seasoning. Pour the consommé into bowls and add the cubes of root vegetables.

Roasted pumpkin soup

I like to use every bit of an ingredient if I can, so I often carve out the pumpkin flesh, leaving a beautiful natural soup bowl for serving the soup. You can also buy a few small pumpkins and use them as individual soup bowls – no china needed and easy to clean up afterwards! Pumpkin seeds are delicious roasted and they make a great snack.

Roasted pumpkin seeds

seeds of 1 pumpkin, washed and dried
1 teaspoon vegetable oil
½ teaspoon ground cinnamon
½ teaspoon ground caraway
salt and pepper

• Preheat the oven to 180°C/Gas 4. Toss the seeds with the oil, spices and seasoning and spread them out on a parchment-lined baking sheet.

• Roast the seeds in the oven for 8–10 minutes, stirring them every few minutes so that they brown evenly.

For crispy pumpkin seeds, dry the seeds in a low oven before roasting.

Stock	Soup
trimmings and skin from the pumpkin	½ pumpkin, peeled and cut into 6 even wedges
700ml chicken stock (see p.258)	1 tablespoon vegetable oil
1 large onion, peeled	1 large onion, peeled and thinly sliced
1 bunch parsley stalks	2 teaspoons ground cinnamon
3–4 sprigs of thyme	
1 cinnamon stick	1 teaspoon caraway seeds
½ head of garlic	1 tablespoon butter
3 celery sticks, roughly chopped	2 tablespoons clear honey
2 carrots, roughly chopped	60ml cream
salt and pepper	salt and pepper

To make the stock
• Put all the pumpkin skin and trimmings into a large pot and cover with chicken stock. Keep the pumpkin seeds back for roasting. Add the rest of the stock ingredients and simmer slowly for at least 1 hour. Leave to rest for 20 minutes and then strain through a sieve.

To make the soup
• Divide the pumpkin wedges into two batches. One batch is for roasting and the other for sweating on top of the stove. Chop the wedges for sweating into 5cm cubes and set aside.

• Heat the oil in a large heavy-bottomed pot over a medium heat. Add the onion, 1 teaspoon of cinnamon and a good pinch of salt, then sweat gently until the onion is very soft. Add the cubes of pumpkin and cook gently until soft. Add enough stock to cover and leave to simmer.

• Meanwhile heat a large frying pan and add the butter. When it begins to foam, put in the large pumpkin wedges, salt and pepper. Allow the pumpkin to colour on both sides (this is important for flavour) and then sprinkle on 1 teaspoon of cinnamon and 1 teaspoon of caraway seeds. Continue to cook, turning occasionally to ensure an even colour.

- After about 5 minutes, add the honey and then put the pumpkin into the oven at 180°C/Gas 4 and roast for 6–8 minutes until it is dark golden brown, soft and well coated in the honey and spice mixture.

- Add the roasted pumpkin to the pot of simmering pumpkin and mix together well, adding more stock if necessary. Leave to cook until the pumpkin is very soft and tender, then add the cream. Check the seasoning and take off heat. Leave the soup to rest for 10 minutes before transferring it to a blender and blitzing until it is very smooth.

To serve

Sprinkle some roasted pumpkin seeds onto each serving. Serve in bowls or a carved-out pumpkin.

The key to a great soup is a good stock.

Pumpkin risotto

Risotto is great family food as it is quick and easy to prepare, and can be flavoured in so many different ways by adding your favourite diced or puréed vegetables. In autumn, I love making risotto with pumpkin and other seasonal vegetables and I always serve it in a big bowl placed in the middle of the table for everyone to help themselves.

1 litre vegetable stock (see p.258)
2 shallots, peeled and finely chopped
2 tablespoons olive oil
200g pumpkin, chopped into 1cm cubes

200g Arborio risotto rice
100ml white wine
1 knob of butter
100g Parmesan cheese, freshly grated
1 sage leaf
salt and pepper

Garnish
4 Jerusalem artichokes
1 teaspoon vegetable oil
3 or 4 pumpkin wedges
salsify crisps (see p.264)
Parmesan cheese

To serve
Serve with the roasted pumpkin and Jerusalem artichokes, salsify crisps and shavings of Parmesan cheese.

To prepare the garnish
- Peel the Jerusalem artichokes. Cut them into wedges and cook in boiling salted water for 8–10 minutes or until soft. Warm the oil in a heavy pan, add the pumpkin and roast in a hot oven for 8–10 minutes. Add the artichokes and roast for another 2 or 3 minutes, then set aside. Prepare the salsify crisps (see p.264).

To make the risotto
- Heat the vegetable stock and leave it to simmer while you begin the risotto. In a separate heavy-bottomed pot, cook the shallots in the olive oil over a medium heat until soft. Season. Now add the pumpkin and season again to taste. Slowly cook the pumpkin until it starts to soften, but do not allow it to colour.

- Add the rice and cook until it turns slightly translucent – 3–4 minutes. Stir in the wine. Once the wine has almost completely evaporated, start adding the simmering stock, a ladleful at a time. Stir after each addition, allowing each ladleful to be almost fully absorbed before adding the next. Continue to add stock until the rice is cooked but still has a slight bite (al dente). This should take about 16 minutes. Check the seasoning again.

- Remove from the heat and add the butter and freshly grated Parmesan. Leave the risotto to rest for 2 minutes and add the chopped sage before serving.

Always use a good-quality risotto rice.
I prefer Arborio.

Leek terrine
with hazelnut dressing

The secret of success with this recipe is to make sure the leeks are thoroughly cleaned, properly cooked and then rolled together when warm as this helps the dish set.

4 leeks
1 handful of sugar
1 handful of salt
3–4 Jerusalem artichokes
lemon juice
fresh herbs

Hazelnut dressing
250g hazelnuts, toasted, skinned and chopped
1 shallot, chopped
1 bunch of chives, chopped

2 tablespoons hazelnut oil
sherry vinegar
salt and pepper

To serve
With the clingfilm still in place, cut the terrine into thick slices, taking care to keep the round shape. Remove the clingfilm. Place a slice of terrine on each plate and top with a spoonful of hazelnut dressing. Spoon some of the artichoke mixture around the terrine and garnish with fresh herbs.

To prepare the leeks
- Trim the leeks and wash them well to remove any excess dirt and sand. Tie them together in a bunch. Bring 2 litres of water to the boil in a large saucepan and add the sugar and salt. Add the leeks and cook until they are very soft, 15–20 minutes.

- Once the leeks are cooked you need to work fast before they cool. Drain them as well as possible, then lay them out in a row on a piece of clingfilm, alternating top to tail. Roll the leeks up in the clingfilm to make a tight log shape. Tie at both ends and pierce the log a few times to let out any more excess liquid. Leave to set in the fridge for at least 6 hours before serving.

To make the hazelnut dressing
- Put the chopped hazelnuts, shallot, chives and hazelnut oil in a bowl and add a splash of sherry vinegar. Mix well and season to taste.

To prepare the Jerusalem artichokes.
- Peel the artichokes, chop into small, even cubes and place in a bowl of water with a squeeze of lemon juice until needed. Bring a small pot of seasoned water to the boil, add the artichokes and cook for 3–4 minutes. Plunge into a bowl of iced water and then drain. Mix the cooked artichoke with two tablespoons of hazelnut dressing and set aside.

When cleaning leeks you only need to cut into the top. There should be no grit in the white part of the leek.

Braised red cabbage

Braised red cabbage is a great accompaniment to many autumn dishes. This recipe for red cabbage cooked with cinnamon and orange works particularly well with game.

½ red cabbage, thinly sliced
100ml port
100ml red wine
2 cinnamon sticks
1 tablespoon vegetable oil
1 large onion, peeled and
  sliced

1 tablespoon fennel seeds
50g golden raisins
2 tablespoons caster sugar
zest of ½ orange
50ml white wine vinegar
salt and pepper

- Place the sliced cabbage in a large bowl and pour in the port and red wine. Add one of the cinnamon sticks and leave the cabbage to marinate for 24 hours. Drain the cabbage and reserve the liquid.

- Heat the oil in a large heavy-bottomed pot over a medium heat. Add the onion, fennel seeds and second cinnamon stick and cook until the onion is very soft and translucent. Add the raisins, sugar and orange zest and mix well. Cover the pot and allow everything to sweat slowly for 20 minutes.

- Add the drained cabbage, white wine vinegar and enough of the reserved marinade liquid just to cover the cabbage. Cook slowly for 45 minutes to an hour, stirring occasionally, until the liquid has reduced and the cabbage is glazed and sticky. Season to taste.

To serve
Place in a large serving dish so everyone can help themselves.

Once cooked, this cabbage dish will keep for at least a week in the fridge and only improve in flavour.

I have used autumn root vegetables for this recipe, but the dish works equally well with spring or summer vegetables. Freeze any leftover stock – it is ideal for poaching fish.

A la Grecque stock
2 tablespoons vegetable oil
½ tablespoon fennel seeds
½ tablespoon coriander
  seeds, crushed
1 large onion, sliced
salt
1 leek, sliced
2 celery sticks, chopped
1 fennel bulb, sliced
125g button mushrooms,
  sliced
2 sprigs thyme
1 bay leaf
½ head of garlic,
zest and juice of 1½ lemons
1 litre white wine

Beetroot
50g rock salt
12 baby beetroot, washed
  and trimmed
2 garlic cloves
zest of ½ orange
2 sprigs of thyme
1 bay leaf

Garnish vegetables
1 teaspoon olive oil
12 florets of cauliflower
1 fennel bulb, cut into
  6 wedges
6 artichoke hearts (tinned
  or fresh)
1 carrot, sliced into
  12 ribbons
6 cooked chestnuts
1 small handful of chives

To serve
Arrange the vegetables on a plate and drizzle with the reduced stock.

To make the à la Grecque stock
- In a large heavy-bottomed stock pot, heat 2 tablespoons of vegetable oil. Add the fennel and crushed coriander seeds and cook for 4–5 minutes to release their flavour.

- Add the onion and a good pinch of salt. Cover the pan and cook over a medium heat until the onions are very soft. Add the leek, celery and fennel and continue to cook for another 6–8 minutes. Then add the mushrooms, thyme, bay leaf, garlic and lemon zest and juice. Cook a few minutes longer, allowing all the ingredients to mix together.

- Pour in the wine and a litre of water, making sure there is enough liquid to cover the vegetables. Cook over a medium to high heat for 30 minutes, stirring frequently. Take the pan off the heat and leave the stock to infuse for another 30 minutes. Pass through a fine sieve, pressing firmly to extract as much liquid as possible. Leave to cool at room temperature and store in a sealed plastic container. This stock freezes well.

To prepare the beetroot

* Heat the oven to 150°C/Gas 2. Lay out a sheet of aluminium foil (A4 size). Sprinkle the rock salt over the foil. Add the beetroot, garlic, orange zest and thyme and fold the foil to make an airtight parcel. Place this in a heavy-bottomed pan and bake for 1½ hours. Remove the parcel from the oven and check the beetroot with a sharp knife to see if they are cooked. If there is still any resistance, put them back in the oven for another 15 minutes. Leave to cool and then peel the beetroot by gently scraping the skin with a knife.

To prepare the garnish vegetables

* In a heavy-bottomed pan, heat the oil and add the cauliflower, fennel and artichokes. Season and add a ladle of grecque stock and cook over a medium to high heat until the stock is reduced by half. Add another ladle of stock, cook for 10–12 minutes, then add the chestnuts, cooked beetroot and ribbons of carrot. Cook for a further 3–4 minutes until the stock has reduced and the vegetables have a sticky glaze. Keep the stock to use as a dressing for the vegetables. Once cooked, the vegetables and stock can be put into an airtight container and kept in the fridge for 4–5 days.

Celeriac, turnip and beetroot gratin

Celeriac, turnip and beetroot are a great combination, but you can use any root vegetables for this gratin – the method remains the same. I often do a carrot and parsnip gratin on a Sunday at home, and pumpkin gratin is also delicious. Always be sure to bake the gratin at a low temperature, as the cream will split if the oven is too hot and the dish will be dry.

20g unsalted butter	½ head of celeriac
150–200ml whipping cream	1 beetroot
pinch of nutmeg	½ turnip
	salt and pepper

To serve
Put the baking dish on the table and let everyone help themselves.

If the gratin starts to get too brown, cover it with foil so the top doesn't burn.

- Butter a 20cm gratin dish and set aside. Bring the cream and nutmeg to a simmer in a saucepan and season with salt and pepper to taste.

- Preheat the oven to 150°C/Gas 2. Peel the celeriac and slice very thinly – preferably with a mandolin. Peel and slice the beetroot and turnip in the same way. Place a layer of celeriac in the buttered dish, top with beetroot and turnip and repeat until all the vegetables are used, finishing with a layer of celeriac.

- Pour the simmering cream mix over the vegetables so that it covers them generously. Place the dish on a baking tray. Bake for about 1½ hours and then check the vegetables are cooked by inserting a sharp knife. If there is any resistance, put the dish back in the oven for 10 minutes.

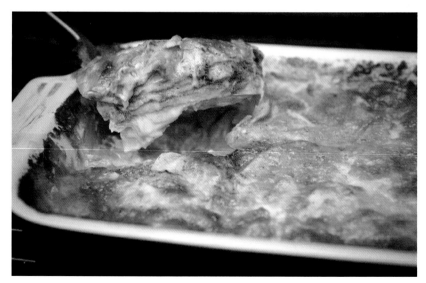

Roasted cod
with broccoli purée

Cod is a wonderful meaty fish, used in many traditional dishes, and in Scotland we're very proud of our country's great history of cod fishing. When buying cod, always ask for a thick piece which will flake beautifully once cooked.

100g broccoli
1 tablespoon butter
120g purple sprouting
  broccoli

1 teaspoon vegetable oil
4 x 200g cod fillets
salt and pepper

- Put a large pan of water on to boil and add salt. Cook the broccoli for 7–8 minutes. Drain, place in the blender while still warm with the butter and blitz for 2–3 minutes until you have a fine purée. Cool as quickly as possible to keep the fresh green colour. Season to taste.

- In another pan, bring some water to the boil and add salt. Trim the purple sprouting broccoli into small florets and blanch for 2–3 minutes. Drain.

- Heat the oven to 180°C/Gas 4. In a large non-stick ovenproof pan, heat the oil and add the seasoned cod, skin side down. Sear for 3–4 minutes. Turn the cod skin upwards, put the pan into the oven and roast the cod for 5 minutes. Then warm the purée and add the cooked broccoli to the pan with the cod to reheat for 1–2 minutes.

To serve
Place some cooked broccoli on each plate and add the cod. Garnish with the broccoli purée.

Orkney

Scotland has, I believe, the world's best shellfish. I get most of my shellfish from the Caithness and Sutherland regions of northern Scotland as well as from Orkney and the Scottish west coast, as the quality of produce there is truly outstanding.

The scallops from Orkney are exceptional. The quality, the size, the flesh are all just right – a perfect scallop. I only ever use hand-dived scallops at The Kitchin and would never consider using anything else. I don't like the thought of dredged scallops – those dragged from the seabed by special nets – and the technique can cause serious damage to the marine life. The fact that dredged scallops usually contain sand should also be a wake-up call to chefs, as the flavours just can't match up with those gathered by divers. The reason why Orkney has such fantastic scallops – 'whoppers', as my fish supplier calls them – is partly due to the inaccessibility of much of the shoreline. The scallops hide underneath rocks, building themselves into the fantastic large delicacies that they are later to become.

Sometimes when the weather is bad, or the ocean is rough, I get a call from my scallop suppliers saying the boat is delayed and my delivery is going to be half an hour later than usual. I don't mind this at all – it just proves how fresh they will be when they arrive at my restaurant. The scallops are always alive when I receive them, still breathing, fresh and snow-white. Same goes for the langoustines, lobster and other shellfish, caught within a matter of hours, taken straight off the boat and stored on ice while they are being delivered to the restaurant. Simply beautiful!

One of the difficulties with shellfish for me as a chef is negotiating a good price for my produce. Most of the shellfish from Scotland is sent directly down to Europe by air or lorry. When working with Pierre Koffmann at La Tante Claire in London and with Guy Savoy in Paris, I discovered that they generally used Scottish shellfish. It was the best there was. This was one of many reasons why I wanted to open a restaurant in Scotland. The thought of getting shellfish straight out of the ocean,

cooking them as fresh as they could be, and introducing my customers to new taste sensations was just too great a temptation.

I enjoy spending time in Orkney with my suppliers to get a better understanding of how they work, and I am always overwhelmed by the consideration shown to all the produce they deal with. I recently brought my supplier and friend Willie Little along. Willie is one of the most knowledgeable people I've ever met and what he doesn't know about the ocean is not worth knowing. Willie has been an enormous help to me since opening the restaurant because of

his skills, knowledge and genuine passion for food, especially fish and shellfish. Willie comes from a family of food lovers and now has his own fish shop in Crieff. I love the stories he tells, such as when his mother used to make jam and leave it hanging in her old tights over the bath to drain and get the consistency just right. I could listen to him all day and he always brings a smile to my face.

Willie and I joined Robert Smith, my scallop-diver in Orkney, and watched as he carefully dived for scallops, picking them up from the bottom of the sea one by one. I realised the risks these guys take every

Orkney

day in the hunt for the perfect produce. 'They should be the size of my palm,' Robert tells me. More than impressive, and probably something that many people don't know when they tuck in to a white-fleshed tasty scallop in a restaurant. During our day in Orkney, Willie and I observed how Robert also collected the lobster creels, and I could not help noticing how much attention he paid to making sure the lobsters and crabs were measured with a special metallic ruler as soon as they came to the surface. The reason for measuring the lobsters and crabs is to check that they are not too small. Any that are,

must be thrown back into the ocean. It's the same with female lobsters carrying thousands of eggs – they, too, are released and thrown straight back into the deep ocean to make sure of many more lobsters. Once again, my philosophy of respecting the produce was confirmed there and then. These guys truly deserve all the recognition they can get – I depend on their hard work and expertise in order to be able to serve top-quality shellfish to my diners.

With most shellfish, such as mussels, clams and razor fish, I use the natural juices from inside the shells when making a hot dish. I do the same with raw oysters, separating the flesh from the shell before collecting the liquid to use as the base for a sauce. Oyster juices can also be used on their own – I simply reduce them, then add butter or cream.

When I worked at Le Louis XV restaurant in Monaco, all the shellfish dishes were prepared and cooked to order – à la minute. We had eight minutes from the moment the order was placed and called in the kitchen to get the dish ready from start to finish. With clams, this meant cooking them the traditional way with white wine, shallots and parsley. We then had to remove the flesh from the shells before straining and reducing the jus, to which we added olive oil or lemon juice. Even when we served a cold shellfish dish, all the preparation of the shellfish, as well as the cooking and cooling, had to be done in the eight minutes. Unbelievably impressive, as was everything about Alain Ducasse's kitchen.

Tasting an oyster fresh from an oyster farm is one of the wonders of the world in my eyes. I know that most people don't ever get to experience the enjoyment of eating a completely fresh, natural oyster just picked out of ice-cold waters, but I am convinced that most fishmongers should be able to get fresh oysters that are less than 24 hours old for a similar taste experience. There is an old saying that you should only eat oysters when there is an 'r' in the month, but as most of the oysters eaten in the UK nowadays are farmed, it's not something I would worry about.

My favourite way of eating oysters is simply to add a squeeze of lemon and a drop of shallot vinegar. Delicious! When opening oysters, check the freshness by touching the outside lining gently.

When the oyster is fresh, it always springs back to the position it was in. I appreciate that there is always a certain risk in eating shellfish, and possibly more so with produce like oysters which are served raw. However, if you know your produce is fresh, the risk should be very limited.

I believe that once you've eaten a really good, fresh oyster you will never forgot the unbelievable taste sensation. My best friend Oliver recently said that oysters taste like running into the sea with your mouth wide open. I totally disagree with him, but it did make me laugh!

Scallops in the shell

1 carrot, chopped
1 leek, sliced
1 teaspoon vegetable oil
2 scallops per person
100g puff pastry
2 egg yolks

White wine sauce
1 tablespoon olive oil
100g shallots, sliced
250ml Noilly Prat vermouth
250ml fish stock (see p.259)

250ml whipping cream
salt and pepper
½ tablespoon grain mustard
1 tablespoon chopped dill

Preparing the white wine sauce

Heat a heavy-bottomed pan on top of the stove and add the oil. Sweat the shallots gently for 3–4 minutes. Add the Noilly Prat and the fish stock and continue to cook until the mixture is reduced and has a syrupy consistency. Add the cream, bring back to the boil and reduce again slightly. Season with salt and pepper, then pass through a strainer or sieve. Add the grain mustard and the chopped dill.

Preparing the scallops

Slip a thin sharp knife between the shells and cut through the large white muscle tab (the abductor muscle) to release one side of the shell. Pry open the shell and pull everything out. Using a spoon, neatly scoop out the meat. Separate the white meat from the outer skirt and roe (the skirt and roe can be kept for making sauces and they freeze well). Rinse the scallops and keep them in the fridge on a paper towel. Rinse the shells and pat them dry.

To serve

Remove the scallop shells from the oven and run a sharp knife all the way around the outer crust. Serve on a bed of seaweed or some rock salt mixed with a little water to stop the shells rocking about and let your guests open the shells themselves.

Assembling the dish

Sweat the carrot and leek in the oil over a low heat. Season and cook until they are soft but not browned. Allow to cool. Take 4 washed shells and divide the leeks and carrots between them. Cut the scallops in half through the middle, season and place 4 pieces on each shell. Cover with 3 tablespoons of white wine sauce and top with the other shells.

Preheat the oven to 200°C/Gas 6. Roll out the puff pastry and cut into thin strips. Place a pastry strip around each scallop to seal the two shells together. Using your fingers, gently press the pastry in place to ensure that the seal is tight and there are no holes. Brush with egg yolk and cook in the hot oven for 8–10 minutes until the pastry is golden brown.

Crab and crab claws
with aïoli

Freshly cooked brown crab, eaten while still warm, must be one of my all-time favourite dishes. Served simply with some brown bread, aïoli and a glass of crisp white wine, this is heaven on a plate for me.

2 crabs with claws
4 extra crab claws
1 tablespoon salt

Aïoli
5 garlic cloves, peeled
3 large egg yolks, at
 room temperature
200ml olive oil

1 tablespoon lemon juice
100ml vegetable oil
salt and pepper

To make the aïoli

- Start by chopping the garlic finely. Sprinkle with salt and, using the back of your knife, crush the garlic into the salt to make a smooth paste. Stir in the egg yolks and leave to rest for 5 minutes. Scrape the mixture into a bowl and add the olive oil a little at a time, whisking constantly.

- Once the aïoli becomes thick, add 2 teaspoons of the lemon juice. Then gradually whisk in more olive oil and last of the lemon juice. Season and then whisk in the vegetable oil. Check again for seasoning and add more salt or lemon if needed.

To cook the crab claws and crab

- Bring a large pan of 2 litres of salted water to the boil. Add the crabs and all the claws and cook for 4–6 minutes. Turn off the heat and leave the crab and claws to cool in the water. This will cook the crabs to perfection.

- Once the crabs and claws have cooled, remove them from the water and twist the claws to separate them. Set aside.

- To remove the centre part of the crab, hold the crab with the head pointing upwards and knock the bottom edge on a chopping board. This should release the middle section, which you should now be able to push up and out of the shell. Discard the outer shell as well as the soft gills attached to the centre part of the body.

- Cut the centre part into four pieces with a pair of sharp kitchen scissors and use a skewer to remove the flesh. Make sure you remove any bits of shell.

To open the crab claws

- Using the back of a knife, crack the claws gently to release the shell from the meat. Remove the flesh from the shells with a skewer. Do the same with the legs.

To serve

I like to serve the crabs and claws whole in a dish on the table so everyone can get stuck in and enjoy picking the meat from the crabs. Put some bowls of lemon water on the table so guests can rinse their fingers.

Crab meat is never the same if it's been kept in the fridge for a few days so always eat crab as fresh as possible.

Oysters
with langoustine mousse

I often serve oysters with this langoustine bisque as I think the flavours go well together, but you can also use a white wine sauce (see p.174). You could also place some finely chopped sautéed vegetables or fresh spinach under the oysters, instead of mousse.

8–10 oysters
langoustine bisque (see p.263)
10 sprigs of seasonal herbs for garnish

Langoustine mousse
100g langoustine meat
100g white fish such as hake, cod or pollack
2 egg whites
300ml whipping cream
pinch of curry powder

salt and pepper
1 tablespoon chopped tarragon
1 tablespoon chopped chives

To make the langoustine mousse
• Place the langoustine meat, fish and egg whites into a food processor and pulse until smooth. With the processor on, gently pour in the cream. Add the curry powder and seasoning, then transfer to a bowl and add the tarragon and chives.

• To check the seasoning and consistency, drop a small teaspoon of the mousse mixture into salted boiling water and cook for 2–3 minutes. Allow to cool, then taste and add extra seasoning if needed.

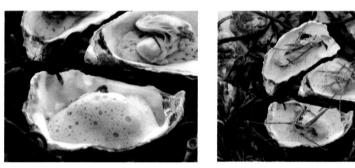

To serve
Froth up the langoustine bisque with a hand whisk and add a tablespoon to each serving. Garnish with seasonal herbs.

To assemble the dish
• Open the oysters, keeping the bottom shells and any natural juices. Using a piping bag, pipe about a tablespoon of the mousse mixture into each oyster shell. Place the filled shells in a vegetable steamer over a pan of simmering water, cover with a lid and steam for 5–6 minutes. Remove and set aside.

• Warm the oysters with their own liquid in a small pan for about 10 seconds, taking care not to let the liquid boil. Place one oyster on each filled shell.

Ninety-nine per cent of oysters are farmed nowadays, so it's no longer true that you can only eat them when there is an 'r' in the month.

Fish pie

You can use any firm fish you like, but pollack, cod, haddock and salmon all work well in a fish pie.

2 litres milk	1kg Maris Piper potatoes	**Béchamel sauce**
600g firm fish fillets, diced into 2cm cubes	2 tablespoons butter	500ml milk
200g smoked fish fillet	salt and pepper	60g butter
4–6 langoustines	1 beaten egg	4 tablespoons flour
2 hard-boiled eggs, peeled and quartered		2 tablespoons grain mustard

To make the béchamel sauce

- Bring the milk up to simmering point in a small pan and set aside. In another pan, melt the butter gently over a medium heat, then add the flour and stir until the mixture is smooth. Now begin adding the milk, a little at a time to avoid lumps. Keep adding milk and stirring until you have a rich creamy sauce. Cook slowly for 5 minutes and then add the grain mustard. Set aside.

Cooking the fish

- Gently heat the 2 litres of milk, taking care that it does not boil over. Add the raw fish fillets and poach in the milk for 3–4 minutes. Add the smoked fish and poach for a further 3–4 minutes. Carefully remove the fish and set aside. Peel the langoustines and gently poach them the same milk for 2–3 minutes. Keep the heads to decorate the pie later. Set the milk aside to use in the mashed potato.

Mashed potato

- Preheat the oven to 200°C/Gas 6. Place the potatoes on a tray and bake in a hot oven until crispy and soft. While still hot, scoop out the flesh, discard the skins, and pass the potato through a sieve to remove any lumps. Heat the milk used for poaching the fish, add the butter and fold into the potato mixture until it is the right consistency.

Making the pie

- Preheat the oven to 190°C/Gas 5. Butter a baking dish and spread a small amount of béchamel on the bottom of the dish. Add the poached fish and quartered eggs, then the remaining béchamel.

- Top with the mashed potatoes, place the langoustine heads into the potato, and brush the top of the pie with beaten egg. Place the pie dish on a baking tray and cook in the preheated oven for 30–40 minutes or until the top is golden brown and bubbling.

To serve

Place the pie on the table so everyone can see how beautiful it is and serve from the dish. Accompany with a nice green salad.

I like to add langoustines to my fish pie as I love
the different texture they introduce.

Potato gnocchi

Using the right type of potato is vital for good gnocchi. The potatoes must be floury and as dry as possible once cooked. I've used this recipe for years and I wish I could tell you that an Italian grandmother passed it on, but that's not the case. The recipe comes from my Scottish friend Dominic Jack.

500g floury potatoes	1 egg
300g rock salt	1 egg yolk
100g flour	salt and pepper

- Preheat the oven to 200°C/Gas 6. Place the potatoes on a bed of salt and bake for 1½ hours. The salt helps to draw out the moisture, leaving a lighter potato. When the potatoes are done, and while they are still hot, scoop out the flesh and pass it through a drum sieve. Sift the flour and set aside.

To serve
Gnocchi are good served with meat or fish or on their own as a vegetarian dish. By adding herbs, olives or different cheeses to the gnocchi you can easily vary the basic recipe.

- Whisk the egg and the egg yolk together. Fold in a small amount of hot potato, in effect tempering the egg. Then fold the egg and potato mix into the rest of the potato. Once it is completely incorporated, fold in the sifted flour, making sure to not let lumps form. Season to taste.

- Knead the mixture into a ball and then shape into rolls about 1.5cm in diameter. Cut these into sections about 2.5cm long.

 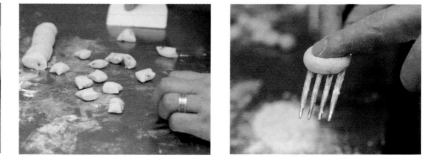

- To shape the gnocchi, hold a fork in one hand and place a piece of dough against the tines of the fork. Using your thumb, press in and down the length of the fork. The gnocchi should curl slightly and take on the impression of the fork (good for catching sauce).

To cook the gnocchi
- Bring a large pan of seasoned water to the boil. When the water is smoking (not bubbling), add the gnocchi and leave them until they float up to the top. Remove immediately and allow to cool. Toss in a tablespoon of vegetable oil so that the gnocchi don't stick together.

Gnocchi freeze very well. They can be frozen after the blanching process and then defrosted at room temperature just before cooking.

Roast mallard
with gnocchi

Mallard is a must on my autumn menu at the restaurant as I adore the unique flavours of the bird. Another wild duck I love at this time of year is teal, which is a much smaller game bird but incredibly tender. I recently cooked teal on Saturday Kitchen, BBC1's live cooking programme, where I prepared the bird using the same method and garnish as here. Teal are smaller than mallard so I recommend serving two birds per person.

1 large mallard, cleaned (ask your butcher!)
vegetable oil
1 apple, cored and cut into wedges
200g girolles (see p.105)
200g gnocchi (see p.182)

8 Brussels sprouts, blanched and halved
braised red cabbage (see p.165)
1 handful watercress
salt and pepper

- Preheat the oven to 240°C/Gas 9. Pat the duck dry with kitchen towel and remove the wishbone, which makes it easier to carve once cooked. To do this, cut down either side of the bone with a sharp knife so you can get your fingers in, then pull and the bone will come away. Season with salt and pepper and don't forget to season inside the cavity.

- Heat some oil in an ovenproof pan and brown the duck on both sides for 2–3 minutes. Place the duck in the oven and cook for 14–16 minutes, depending on its size. Remove from oven and leave to rest for 5 minutes.

- While the duck is resting, sauté the apple in a teaspoon of oil, then add the cooked girolles and gnocchi. Season, add the Brussels sprouts and cook everything together for a couple of minutes.

Accompaniments

- Duck works well with many different accompaniments. I like to serve it with some braised red cabbage and watercress, but it also tastes great with a celeriac, turnip and beetroot gratin (see p.168) or just some mashed potato.

To serve

Place the duck on a serving dish with the vegetables around it and carve at the table for that extra wow factor.

The mallard season is from September to the end of January so if you eat it at other times you know it's been frozen.

Game pithivier

This dish represents traditional French cooking at its best in my opinion. It is incredibly tasty, as the game filling or farce cooks in the pastry, and the butter adds that characteristic flavour. To check that the seasoning of the filling is right before you cook it, take a full teaspoon, fry it quickly and taste to make sure that it is exactly as you want. If you don't have enough game trimmings for this dish you can also use pork or bacon trimmings, which are both quite subtle and will add the necessary moisture. Always try to eat this the day it's made, as that is when it is at its very best.

60g butter
1½ onions, peeled and diced
2 garlic cloves, crushed
8 sprigs of thyme
150ml brandy

150ml port
300g venison trimmings
100g hare trimmings
250g pork fat
100g pork belly

150g game livers
150g foie gras
2–3 sheets of frozen puff pastry, 2mm thick
1 egg, beaten
salt and pepper

To make the filling

- Melt the butter in a pan and gently cook the onions and garlic until they are very soft and translucent. Mix in the thyme. Add the brandy and port and continue to cook until the alcohol has evaporated. Spread the mixture out on a plate and leave to cool.

- Once the onion is cool, mix with the venison, hare, pork fat and belly, livers and foie gras. Mince this mixture and place in a large bowl. Season with salt and pepper. It's important to check the seasoning at this point. The best way to do this is to fry small amount (basically a mini-burger) in a frying pan until cooked through and then taste it. Correct the seasoning if necessary.

To assemble the pithiviers

- Preheat the oven to 180°C/Gas 4. Lay out the pastry and cut out four 12cm discs for the bases and four 16cm discs for the tops. Lay the pastry bases on separate pieces of baking parchment to make the pithiviers easier to handle.

- Place a small amount of the filling mix in the centre of each pastry base. Make it as round as possible, for a neat finished product. Then lay the pastry tops over the filling, pressing the edges together firmly to enclose the meat mix and making sure there are no air pockets.

Take your time when scoring the pastry as the lines will stand out once cooked and it will be too late to change.

- Brush the pastry with beaten egg and place in the fridge for 15–20 minutes to rest the pastry. Very carefully score the top with the tip of a small knife, starting at the centre and curving round to the base. Make a small hole at the centre to allow steam and excess moisture escape.

- Bake in the preheated oven for 15–20 minutes or until golden brown.

To serve
A pithivier is a meal itself so just serve with a green salad to eat afterwards.

Stuffed cabbage

This is traditionally known as 'choux farci de Gascogne' and is one of the most flavoursome dishes I know. The cabbage leaves protect the meat, holding it all together, and bring incredible flavours to the finished dish. It goes well with game, too.

1 large green cabbage
crepinette (caul fat)

Stuffing
60g butter
1½ onions, peeled and diced
2 garlic cloves, crushed
3 sprigs of thyme
200ml brandy

400g venison trimmings, chopped small
150g wild mallard livers and hearts, diced
300g pork fat, chopped small
salt
pepper
2 eggs

Braising liquid
8 slices of pancetta, diced
vegetable oil
3 carrots, peeled and diced
1 onion, peeled and diced
4 celery sticks, diced
100ml brandy
100ml Madeira
1 bouquet garni (see p.265)
500ml veal stock (see p.260)

To make the stuffing
- Melt the butter in a pan and gently cook the onions and garlic until soft and translucent. Mix in the thyme. Add the brandy and reduce until the alcohol has boiled away. Transfer the mixture to a plate and leave to cool.

- Once the onion mixture is cool, fold it into the meats and mince. Season with salt and pepper and fold in the eggs. It's important to check the seasoning at this point. The best way to do this is to fry small amount (basically a mini-burger) in a frying pan until cooked through and then taste it to make sure it is as you want. Correct the seasoning if necessary.

Preparing the braising liquid
- In a large heavy-bottomed pot, cook the pancetta in a little vegetable oil until golden. Next add the carrots and cook until evenly coloured. Then add the diced onion and celery and leave to sweat until soft. Check the seasoning. Add the brandy and Madeira and cook until all the alcohol has boiled away.

Toss in the bouquet garni and add veal stock to cover. Let the mixture come to the boil, then take off the heat. Set aside until you are ready to braise the cabbage.

Stuffing the cabbage

Choose the best leaves of the cabbage – you will need 8–10. Discard the first few outer ones as they tend to be bitter and tough. Blanch the leaves in salted, rapidly boiling water for 3–4 minutes, until soft and pliable, then plunge them into a bowl of ice water. Drain and pat dry between 2 pieces of kitchen towel.

Preheat the oven to 150°C/Gas 2. Remove the large rib from the centre of each leaf to make it easier to roll up. Pack each cabbage leaf with a small amount of stuffing, making sure the veins of the leaf are on the inside. Carefully pull the sides of the leaf around the stuffing to make a round, neat parcel. Gently wrap this in enough crepinette (caul fat) to hold it securely so the parcel stays together while cooking.

Place the finished cabbage parcels in a deep ovenproof baking dish and cover with braising liquid. Braise in the preheated oven for 45–60 minutes, until the parcels are cooked through and the braising liquid has reduced slightly.

To serve

Place a stuffed cabbage leaf in the centre of a bowl and pour some reduced braising liquid on top. Serve with some vegetable crisps (see p.264) and vegetables from the braising liquid.

Roast pheasant
with apple and Calvados sauce

Be careful not to overcook pheasant, as it will turn very dry and stringy. Always do the skewer test to ensure it is cooked to perfection. Any leftover meat from the roast pheasant can be picked off the bone and made into a delicious casserole.

1 pheasant	1 apple, quartered	4 shallots, sliced
vegetable oil	1 teaspoon vegetable oil	brandy
1 carrot, peeled and roughly chopped into 2cm dice	4 cooked chestnuts	Calvados
	salt and pepper	240ml chicken stock (see p.258)
100g pancetta, roughly chopped into 2cm dice	**Apple and Calvados sauce**	30ml whipping cream
4 sprigs of thyme		salt and pepper
1 bay leaf	1 apple, peeled and chopped	

To roast the pheasant

* Preheat the oven to 200°C/Gas 6. Make sure the pheasant is at room temperature before you start to cook and season it well, inside and out. Take out the wishbone to make it easier to carve (see p.184). Heat a tablespoon of oil in a large heavy-bottomed ovenproof pan and sear the pheasant until it is golden brown on all sides. Add the chopped carrot and pancetta and the thyme sprigs and bay leaf.

* Make sure the pheasant is breast side down and put it in the hot oven to roast for 8–10 minutes. Flip to the other breast and roast for another 8–10 minutes. Then put the pheasant on its back and cook for another 6 minutes, depending on the size. A good way to check that the bird is cooked is to insert a skewer into the thigh, them remove it, looking carefully at what comes out. If the liquid is clear the pheasant is cooked.

* Remove the bird from the oven and leave to rest on a warm dish, breast upwards, for at least 10 minutes before carving. Set aside the roasted carrots and pancetta.

To prepare the roast apple

* Cut the apple into quarters, removing the core but keeping it aside for the sauce. Heat a frying pan and add the oil. Add the quartered apple and cook until golden – this will take 4–5 minutes. Add the chestnuts and cook for a further 1–2 minutes and then set aside.

Use the core and trimmings from the apple
for the sauce – they are full of flavour.

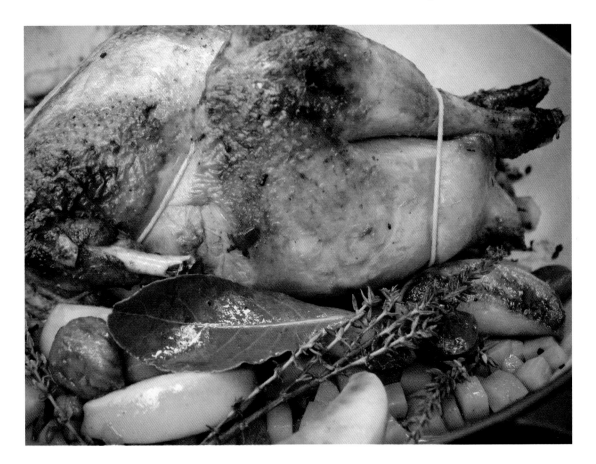

To make the apple and calvados sauce

- Once the pheasant has been set aside to rest, pour off the excess fat from the roasting pan and put it on the stove over a medium heat. Add the apple and shallots and sweat until softened. Deglaze the pan with a healthy splash of brandy and Calvados. Reduce until the alcohol has almost boiled away, then add the chicken stock and simmer until slightly thickened. Add the cream and continue to reduce until the sauce coats the back of a spoon. Pass the sauce through a sieve and check the seasoning.

To serve

Take the legs and breasts off the pheasant and serve with the roasted apple, chestnuts and the apple and Calvados sauce.

Venison loin
with pumpkin gnocchi

I use roe deer and red deer in the restaurant. I prefer the gamier flavour of red deer, but roe often seems to be more tender. I always ask my game dealer to hang my venison for 10–12 days, to ensure the meat is tender and full of flavour.

4 x 200g venison loins, trimmed and ready to cook	200ml venison sauce (see p.261)	**Pumpkin gnocchi**
vegetable oil	1 teaspoon chopped shallot	500g pumpkin, cut into large pieces
200g pumpkin	1 teaspoon chopped chives	100g flour
60g cooked girolles (see p.105)	200g fresh spinach	1 egg
	salt and pepper	1 egg yolk
		vegetable oil
		salt and pepper

To serve

Slice the rested venison. Place some pumpkin and gnocchi mix in the centre of each plate with some spinach. Arrange some slices of venison on top and finish with venison sauce.

To make the gnocchi

● Preheat the oven to 150°C/Gas 2. Put the pumpkin pieces on a roasting tray and roast for about 1½ hours until very soft, ridding them of excess moisture. Pass the cooked pumpkin through a drum sieve to remove any lumps.

● Sift the flour and set aside. Whisk the egg and egg yolk in a bowl and then fold in a small amount of hot pumpkin, in effect tempering the egg. Then add this into the rest of the pumpkin. Once it is thoroughly incorporated, fold in the sifted flour, taking care not to allow any lumps to form.

● Knead the mixture into a ball and then shape into rolls about 1.5cm in diameter. Cut these into sections about 2.5cm long. To shape the gnocchi, hold a fork in one hand and place a piece of dough against the tines of the fork. Using your thumb, press in and down the length of the fork (see p.182). The gnocchi should curl slightly and take on the impression of the fork (good for catching sauce). Drop these pieces into seasoned boiling water and leave until they begin to float. Remove immediately and allow to cool. Toss the gnocchi in a little oil so they don't stick together.

To prepare the venison loins

● Preheat the oven to 200°C/Gas 6. Season the venison. Heat a teaspoon of vegetable oil in a heavy pan and sear the venison. Finish in the hot oven, cooking for 6 or 7 minutes for medium-rare meat. Take the meat out of the oven and set aside to rest.

Always serve venison pink,
or it can be very tough.

To finish
- Cut the pumpkin flesh into fat slices. Heat a teaspoon of vegetable oil in a non-stick frying pan and cook the pumpkin until golden brown. Add the gnocchi and girolles and warm everything through together. Finish with a spoonful of venison sauce and a teaspoon each of shallots and chives. Toss through until glazed. Briefly cook the spinach until wilted and season.

Roast pork belly

Roast pork belly must be my favourite Sunday lunch. I adore the crisp crunchiness of the crackling and the moisture of the meat. The fat from the belly gives the meat an outstanding flavour.

1kg belly of pork, skin on and boned	4–6 potatoes, cut into 6 wedges	4 cloves of garlic
salt and pepper	3 large carrots, cut in half	4 sprigs of rosemary
		250ml chicken stock (see p.258)

To roast the pork

- Preheat the oven to 200°C/Gas 6. Season the pork very liberally with salt and pepper and place it skin side down in a roasting tray. Put a heavy ovenproof pot on top – this helps to keep the belly flat and results in better crackling.

- Place in the preheated oven and roast for 1 hour. Then turn the heat down to 180°C/Gas 4 and flip the belly skin side up. By now the skin should be a even golden brown. Continue to roast for 45 minutes to 1 hour. Remove from the oven and allow the meat to rest for 10 minutes.

To prepare the vegetables

- Parboil the potatoes in a large pot of salted water for 7–8 minutes. Drain and leave to cool at room temperature. Place them in a bowl and toss around to fluff the edges – this helps to make the potatoes really crispy.

- About 45 minutes before the pork is due to be ready, add the potatoes, carrots, garlic and rosemary to the roasting pan. Turn the vegetables occasionally to make sure they colour evenly and absorb the cooking juices of the pork.

- Remove the pork and vegetables from the pan and keep warm. Deglaze the pan with the chicken stock, heat through and serve with the meat.

To serve

Carve the pork with a heavy knife that can cut through the crackling. Serve on top of the roasted vegetables with the cooking juices.

Try cooking pork from rare breeds farmed near you. The difference in flavour from the supermarket pork is remarkable.

Pink peppercorn bavarois
with bramble syrup

This dish is easy to make but the idea of using peppercorns in a dessert will surprise and delight your guests.

Bavarois
250ml milk
1 tablespoon pink
  peppercorns
100g sugar
4 eggs, separated
2 leaves gelatin
100g whipping cream

Bramble syrup
150g blackberries
100ml water
100g sugar
juice of ½ lemon

Garnish
almond tuiles, optional
  (see p.136)

To serve
Remove the serving glasses from the fridge and decorate each one with an almond tuile.

To make the bavarois
- Heat the milk with the pink peppercorns. In a separate bowl, whisk the sugar with the egg yolks. Gradually pour the warm milk over the sugar and egg mix while constantly whisking. Remove from the heat and leave to cool before passing through a fine sieve. Set aside.

- Put the gelatin leaves to soak in a little cold water. Whisk the cream until it forms soft peaks and in a separate bowl whisk the egg whites until stiff. Remove the gelatin from the cold water and warm it over a low temperature until it begins to melt. Add the gelatin to the bavarois mix and then gently fold in the whipped cream, followed by the egg whites. Spoon some bavarois into each serving glass.

To make the bramble syrup
- Put all the ingredients for the syrup into a pan and bring to the boil. Remove from the heat and blitz in a food blender. Pass the mixture through a fine sieve, then pour into a clean pan and reduce until it becomes a syrup. Cool and pour on top of the pink peppercorn bavarois in the serving glasses. Leave to set in the fridge for at least 45 minutes.

This dish can be prepared and put in the fridge a few hours before serving.

Mulled wine

Many people associate mulled wine with Christmas, but for me it is linked with cold autumn days – perfect for bonfire night! I love to take a thermos of mulled wine on a late autumn trip into the woods to enjoy nature's colours before the weather gets too cold.

1 bottle red wine	2–3 star anise
rind of 1 orange	250g sugar (or to taste)
1 large cinnamon stick	100g almonds
1 teaspoon grated nutmeg	100g raisins

Place all the ingredients, except the almonds and raisins, in a large pot and bring to a gentle boil. Turn down the heat and simmer for up to 20 minutes. Remove from the heat and leave to infuse for another 20 minutes. Strain and set aside.

To serve
When you are ready to drink the wine, reheat and pour it into small glasses or cups. Serve with some finely chopped almonds and raisins.

Poached pears
with crème fraîche mousse

This dish can be served warm or cold. Once the pears have been poached you can keep them covered in the syrup for several days and they will still taste delicious.

4 pears
1 lemon
1 bottle mulled wine (see p.197)
star anise

Crème fraîche mousse
250ml crème fraîche
250ml whipping cream
sugar to taste
zest of 1 lemon

To serve
Warm the pears through in the mulled wine. Place each pear in a large shallow bowl, pour over some mulled wine and add a large spoonful of mousse.

To prepare the pears
- Peel the pears with a vegetable peeler and rub with the cut lemon. Place the pears in a pan, cover with mulled wine and slowly bring up to a simmer. Poach the pears slowly until tender, then remove from the liquid and leave to cool.

To make the crème fraîche mousse
- Place all the ingredients in a bowl and whisk to firm peaks. Leave to set in the fridge for 15 minutes before serving.

Rub the peeled pears with a cut lemon to stop them going brown.

Apple pie

Apple pie is one of my favourite autumn puddings and is best made using apples you've picked yourself from your own or a friend's garden. Every autumn I'm given loads of apples by my friend Moira so I can store some for the winter months.

2 large cooking apples, peeled and cored
100g sugar
2 tablespoons flour
1 teaspoon cinnamon

2 large Granny Smith apples, peeled and cored
1 egg, beaten

Sweet pastry
500g flour
100g icing sugar
350g unsalted butter
1 egg

To prepare the filling
Chop the cooking apples and put them in a pan with the sugar and flour (adding flour helps to retain juices and so stops the crust getting soggy when cooking). Add 75ml of water and cook over a low heat until the apple is soft, then add the cinnamon and mix with a wooden spoon to make a smooth purée. Slice the Granny Smith apples and fold the slices into the purée.

To make the pastry
Sift the flour and sugar together. Pulse them with the butter in a food processor until the mix resembles breadcrumbs. Mix in the egg until the dough clings together, then knead gently. Flatten the dough into a round, and divide into 2 pieces. Wrap each in clingfilm and chill in the fridge for 15 minutes.

Assembling the pie
Preheat the oven to 230°C/Gas 8 and grease a 23cm pie dish. Roll out one piece of dough into a circle with a diameter about 10cm bigger than your pie dish. Use this to line the pie dish, then spoon in the apple mixture. Roll out the second piece of dough to the same size and lay it carefully over the pie. Tuck the edges of the top crust under the lower crust and press them together. Cut a few vents in the top crust with a sharp paring knife and brush the pastry with the beaten egg.

Place the pie on the lowest rack of the preheated oven and bake for 10 minutes. Lower the temperature to 180°C/Gas 4 and bake for another 25–30 minutes.

To serve
Dust with some icing sugar and serve with whipped cream or vanilla ice cream.

Putting a hole in the top of the pastry allows
the steam to escape from the pie.

Orange pudding

This fantastic orange pudding is an old family recipe and makes a wonderful autumn dessert. Be sure to pour on the orange reduction as soon as you take the pudding out of the oven – the sponge absorbs the juice better when warm.

200ml orange juice (3–4 oranges)	zest of 5 oranges	7 egg whites
150g butter, softened, plus extra for greasing dish	6 egg yolks	130g orange marmalade
300g caster sugar	220g flour	90ml milk
	1 tablespoon baking powder	3 tablespoons orange reduction (see p.264)

To serve

Divide the pudding into portions, or unmould individual puddings, and drizzle on the remaining orange reduction. Serve with cream or ice cream.

- Bring the orange juice to the boil and continue to boil until it is reduced by half. Set aside to cool.

- Preheat the oven to 190°C/Gas 5 and butter a large pudding dish or individual moulds. Using a food mixer or electric whisk, beat the butter, 100g of the sugar and the orange zest until smooth. Fold in the egg yolks and set aside. Sift the flour and baking powder together.

- Whisk the egg whites with the rest of the sugar until stiff. Fold in the marmalade and the reduced orange juice. Carefully fold the butter mixture into this meringue mix. Next fold in flour and baking powder, then slowly stir in the milk. Pour the mixture into the pudding dish or moulds, until three quarters full.

- Bake for 30–45 minutes for a large pudding, or 15–20 minutes if using individual moulds. Leave to rest for 5 minutes, then glaze with orange reduction, keeping some back for serving.

Pumpkin crème brûlée

Pumpkin is not often used in desserts in Britain, but it is much more popular in southern Europe, especially Italy. I came up with this idea when experimenting with my crème brûlée recipe and the result was pump-tastic! You will need four 200g ramekin dishes.

100g pumpkin flesh, cut into small pieces
225ml whipping cream
25g sugar

4 egg yolks
4 tablespoons Demerara sugar

- In a small heavy-bottomed pan, slowly cook the pumpkin with the cream and sugar until very soft. Cool, then transfer to a blender and blitz until smooth.

- Preheat the oven to 100°C/Gas ½. Whisk the egg yolks in a clean bowl and slowly add the puréed pumpkin, making sure it is thoroughly incorporated.

- Pour the mixture into the ovenproof dishes, place them on a baking tray and cover with aluminium foil. Bake for 30–40 minutes until the mixture is just set, then leave to cool for about 30 minutes at room temperature. Once cooled, leave to set completely in the fridge.

To serve
Sprinkle each ramekin with a tablespoon of Demerara sugar and then brown with a blowtorch or under the grill until the top is crisp and crunchy and a nice golden colour. If you like, decorate with balls of pumpkin, mint leaves and a few squares of chocolate.

Cooking crème brûlée at a low temperature ensures the right consistency. It does take longer, but the result is well worth it.

Sea buckthorn posset

Sea buckthorn was first mentioned to me by a Swedish friend, as the berries grow widely around Sweden. Shortly afterwards, my forager Ben brought some to the restaurant for me to try and I have used them ever since. The orange berries grow in abundance all along the Scottish shores and they not only have a super-high vitamin content but also taste delicious. Their sweet, honey-like flavour, with a hint of citrus and exotic fruits, gives them a truly exclusive character which is extraordinary on its own or with chocolate.

100g sea buckthorn berries
1 tablespoon sugar
375ml cream

130g sugar
dark chocolate

- Put the berries and tablespoon of sugar into a pan with 2 tablespoons of water, bring to the boil and simmer for 10 minutes. Leave to rest for 10 minutes. Pass through a fine sieve, keeping the liquid and discarding the seeds and pulp.

- Bring the cream and 130g of sugar to the boil and add to the sea buckthorn liquid. Pour the mixture into a bowl resting over a bowl of ice and stir until it starts to set. The acidity in the berries helps to set the mixture naturally. Pour into moulds or glasses and leave to chill in the fridge for at least an hour.

To serve
Top each posset with some of the remaining sea buckthorn liquid and shavings of dark chocolate.

Never pick berries to eat if you are unsure of what they are. Always research carefully before picking to avoid any dangerous lookalikes.

Winter

My cooking in winter is, as always, a reflection of the season. The dishes are naturally heavier, the sauces darker, and I especially enjoy experimenting with new game dishes. Nowadays we can get hold of most types of produce at any time of year, but I like to maintain the classic procedures and techniques and base my cooking around seasonal produce. In winter, as at other times of year, local seasonal ingredients are best, as the foods have a natural affinity.

Many of the traditional recipes I love to cook come from the days when meat and fish had to be cured and prepared to store for the harsh winter months, and some have been passed down through the generations. Although I enjoy experimenting with dishes and adding my own personal touches, there are certain traditional dishes, such as woodcock, hare à la royale, coq au vin and braised oxtail, that must never be changed as they represent the true fundamentals of classic cooking.

The woodcock dish on page 226 for example is one I learned to prepare when working with Pierre Koffmann and Alain Ducasse. These remarkable little birds fly in from Scandinavia or from as far away as Russian and Latvia to escape the icy winters. Woodcock is an absolute pleasure to prepare and I take immense care with the whole cooking process in order to maximise that special flavour. As soon as the birds are available I can't wait to put them on my menu at the restaurant, and other than adding my own touch with the garnish, I follow the classic recipe and use the intestines to create a delicious pâté and the bones for a sauce. I always serve the bird with the head cut in half as woodcock brains are a true delicacy. I feel it is my duty as a chef to share what I have been taught with my chefs and to keep the traditional methods of cooking going, but I also like to search for ways of developing dishes and incorporating them into my world through the methods of cooking I enjoy.

207

Winter

I love to cook winter ducks, such as teal and mallard, as well as hare and roe deer in winter. These meats have outstanding flavour and they can be used in stews, casseroles or pies. Many of the procedures in winter recipes can be quite complex and in a restaurant kitchen it's well known that the chef who cooks the meat is in for a tough few months as the early winter kicks in. At The Kitchin it is not unusual for us to have pheasant, grouse, hare, partridge, mallard, teal, woodcock and venison all on the menu on the same day in winter. Cooking game and mastering all the techniques and procedures of the different dishes can be a great strain to a young chef or anyone without the right skills, but it is incredibly rewarding.

Game is amazingly versatile and there are a number of ways to extract the different flavours through methods of cooking. Depending on where on the animal the meat has been taken from, the flavour can vary greatly. Never be afraid of using different parts of the animal in the same dish, but always remember that some parts might require different techniques of cooking for the best result. The prime cut of game – the breast or fillet of birds such as woodcock and grouse, or the loin of hare and venison – is usually served pink but often accompanied with braised meat to create a different texture and add excitement to the finished dish. I often confit duck legs, for example, and serve them with duck breasts because they go so well together. I also like to braise the legs of hare and use them as filling in ravioli or in a game pie, as I think the exceptional taste of hare gives just the right balance when combined with pasta or pastry.

The basis of many winter dishes is quite straightforward and simple and the technique I use is

Winter

one that can be applied not just to game, but to most meat dishes for exceptional flavours. Cooking a daube of beef or a coq au vin is a two-day process but quite simple once you know how. A mistake that many cooks make is to use the red wine from the marinade when cooking the meat. By doing so, all the bitterness and blood from the meat leads to a dish that will taste simply bitter. What I always do after marinating the meat is to drain off the wine and discard it together with the vegetables as they are no longer good to use. I prepare fresh vegetables and use another bottle of wine for cooking the dish. The flavour you get in the meat is outstanding and tasty and exactly how you want it. By experimenting and

adding different herbs or spices or maybe more garlic you can easily fashion new taste sensations. I often use this method for cooking not only different cuts of beef, but also for chicken, hare and duck legs. The cooking process becomes easy once you learn how to extract flavours, and by understanding the importance of basic cooking you can easily see how my techniques can be applied to many dishes.

Nothing beats a good home-made stew on a cold day and I usually serve it with variations of potatoes, pasta or home-made polenta as they all absorb the robust sauce and complement the rich taste. Potatoes are such a staple part of the British diet and they feature in many of our best-loved dishes such as Lancashire hotpot, Irish stew and shepherd's pie as well as gratins. I love mashed potatoes with a rich braised oxtail in winter.

Adding winter root vegetables such as parsnips, celeriac and Jerusalem artichokes to meat and game dishes helps to give an unusual blend of flavours and lightens the dishes, ensuring they are not too heavy. It is hard to image that root vegetables used to be peasant food in the old days and were something that many used to feed their animals with. Root vegetables grow incredibly well in our Scottish climate and should be an obvious choice in our winter cooking. And as in autumn, I like to use fruits with my heavier game recipes to help balance the dish. I especially favour winter apples, quince and plums as they are all in their prime in Scotland during the winter months. Juniper berries and cranberries made into jams or jellies make excellent accompaniments to many meat dishes at this time of year, and I also use chestnuts, hazelnuts and walnuts in my cooking as they add interesting textures on the plate.

Winter for me is one of the most unpredictable seasons in my cooking year, simply because of the difficult weather conditions in Scotland. As much as I

210

value and respect my suppliers and know they do anything to source my produce, certain things are out of their control. When the weather is poor I often wonder if the boats will be going out. I have the utmost respect for the fishermen, lobstermen, scallop divers and others who work to find the produce I need for my kitchen, but even more so when the weather conditions are unbearable. It is only since returning to Scotland and building up my relationship with my suppliers I have fully realised what incredibly hard work fishing really is. You can never control the ocean, nor fully predict the weather, and you can certainly never be sure of your next catch.

In the month of December I always make sure I go to the Christmas market in Edinburgh. They do a fantastic job of showcasing some excellent Scottish produce, such as pork and sausages, and I especially enjoy sampling some mulled wine and finding the chestnut stand.

Christmas in the Kitchin household is always a battle between modern Scottish and my wife's Swedish traditions, but somehow we have managed to come to an arrangement that the whole family enjoys. We prepare the Swedish dishes such as herring, gravlax, and ham with mustard as well as the traditional goose, turkey and other delights.

I love to see the fridge full to the brim the day before Christmas, knowing it will all disappear in the following days. I adore cold ham, turkey and goose and I often create new dishes from the leftovers. Ideas for dishes come in moments when you least expect and sometimes I've had brilliant discoveries by going through the fridge and using up what's there.

To some chefs, the last day of the shooting season, January 31, cannot arrive soon enough. The winter season is a tough time for any chef because of the hard work involved in many dishes, but definitely one of the most rewarding. But as much as I love my winter cooking, there is always a part of me longing for the lighter and longer days of spring.

Michaela's scrambled eggs

Sunday breakfast is a real treat for me. The restaurant is closed and I can take the chance to relax properly and spend some quality time with my wife and son. I'm always tired from the week, but I like to get up early to catch Match of the Day with my son and flick through the Sunday papers. We always make a big breakfast, which can turn into quite a feast. I especially enjoy cheesy scrambled eggs which we eat with some fresh rustic bread from the local deli and a few slices of Parma ham. This is my wife's recipe and she insists on using no butter at all, but I will admit that it does taste delicious!

To serve
Spoon the eggs onto the grilled sourdough and garnish with chopped chives and the rest of the cheese. Serve with the roasted tomatoes and some slices of Parma ham.

C eggs
2 tablespoons milk
4 slices sourdough or other rustic bread
100g Mull Cheddar, shaved with a vegetable peeler
salt and pepper
1 tablespoon chopped chives
6 slices Parma ham

Roast vine tomatoes
4 small bunches of cherry tomatoes on the vine
1 tablespoon extra virgin olive oil
1 teaspoon balsamic vinegar
sprig of thyme
Maldon sea salt
cracked black pepper

To prepare the roast vine tomatoes

- Preheat the oven to 190°C/Gas 5. Place the vine tomatoes on a sheet of aluminium foil and drizzle with the oil and vinegar. Add the thyme and a pinch of salt and pepper. Fold the foil over the tomatoes to make a parcel, place on a baking sheet and cook in the preheated oven for 15 minutes. Set aside in a warm place until the eggs are ready.

To cook the eggs

- Whisk the eggs and milk in a bowl until light and fluffy. Grill the sourdough. Warm a large non-stick pan over a medium heat. Add the eggs, straight into the pan, and stir with a wooden spoon until they are just beginning to set. Next, add a few shavings of cheese and continue to mix, allowing the cheese to slowly melt into the eggs. Take the pan off the heat and stir until everything is just set and creamy. Season to taste.

Gnocchi
with Scottish blue cheese

Serves 4

This is the ultimate comfort food recipe which I first had at my friend Dominic's house, when we worked together at Gleneagles many years ago. His mother Alison has since cooked this dish whenever I visit and I still enjoy it just as much.

500g floury potatoes	**Garnish**	**Blue cheese sauce**
500g rock salt	8 spring onions	150ml whipping cream
100g flour	3 firm red tomatoes, diced	100ml milk
1 egg		300g blue cheese
1 egg yolk		1 teaspoon chopped chives
vegetable oil		1 teaspoon chopped shallots
salt and pepper		black pepper

To prepare the gnocchi
- Preheat the oven to 200°C/Gas 6. Place the potatoes on a bed of salt and bake for 1½ hours. (The salt helps to draw out moisture, leaving a lighter potato to work with.) While the potatoes are still hot – this is important – scoop out all the flesh and pass it through a drum sieve. Sift the flour and set aside.

- Whisk the egg and the egg yolk together. Fold in a small amount of hot potato, in effect tempering the egg. Then fold the egg and potato mix into the rest of the potato. Once it is completely incorporated, fold in the sifted flour, making sure to not let lumps form. Season to taste.

- Knead the mixture into a ball and then shape into rolls about 1.5cm in diameter. Cut these into sections about 2.5cm long.

- To shape the gnocchi, hold a fork in one hand and place a piece of dough against the tines of the fork. Using your thumb, press in and down the length of the fork – look at the pictures on page 182. The gnocchi should curl slightly and take on the impression of the fork – good for catching sauce.

To cook the gnocchi
- Bring a large pan of seasoned water to the boil. When the water is smoking (not bubbling), add the gnocchi and leave them until they float up to the top. Remove immediately and allow to cool. Toss in a tablespoon of vegetable oil to stop the gnocchi sticking together.

Blue cheese sauce
- Warm the cream and milk together in a saucepan until just simmering. Add the blue cheese and stir until melted. Finish with chives, shallots and a twist of black pepper. Check the seasoning.

To serve
Warm a large pan over medium heat and add 1 teaspoon of vegetable oil. Add enough gnocchi for 4 people (12 pieces each) and sauté until golden brown on all sides. Add the spring onions and diced tomatoes. Pour in the blue cheese sauce, toss to coat and divide between 4 bowls. Serve immediately.

Caramelised chicory tatin
with Stornoway black pudding

The bitterness of the chicory works very well with the sweetness of the caramel in this tatin recipe. You will need four round metal moulds, about 4cm in diameter. Grease them well with butter.

butter for greasing moulds
150g caster sugar for lining moulds
4 heads of chicory
1 tablespoon butter
150g caster sugar

1 teaspoon salt
1 sheet puff pastry (about A4 size)
1 egg
extra caster sugar for dusting pastry

Garnish
4 x 100g slices of Stornoway or other good quality black pudding
1 teaspoon vegetable oil
salad leaves

- Using a pastry brush, butter the moulds. Sprinkle the sugar into them, making sure all the inner surfaces are covered. Put the moulds under a preheated grill to caramelise the sugar and butter, then set aside.

- Trim off the bottoms of the chicory and cut them lengthwise, removing the centre core. Slice into 2cm strips. Heat the tablespoon of butter in a large heavy-bottomed frying pan and gently cook the chicory strips. Season them with the 150g caster sugar and a teaspoon of salt and continue cooking slowly until the chicory is soft and a golden caramel colour. Pour the chicory mix into a colander and leave for 5 minutes to drain any excess liquid.

- Lay out the puff pastry and, using a 9cm round cutter, cut out 4 circles. Prick each circle all over with a fork. Leave the pastry to rest in the fridge.

- Preheat the oven to 190°C/Gas 5. When the chicory is cool enough to handle, arrange in neat strips in the moulds. Place the pastry circles on top and gently push down and tuck in the edges. Brush with beaten egg and dust with a teaspoon of caster sugar. This helps to seal the pastry and make a nice crunchy base.

- Place the tatins on a baking tray and bake in the preheated oven for 20–25 minutes or until the puff pastry is a deep golden colour. Remove from the oven and loosen the pastry edges. Turn out the tarts, upside down, so the pastry becomes the base under the chicory.

To cook the black pudding
- Heat the vegetable oil in a non-stick pan. Add the slices of black pudding and fry until crisp on both sides – 3 or 4 minutes. Keep warm.

To serve
Serve the warm tatins with the black pudding and garnish with a handful of salad leaves.

Once you start cutting the chicory you must work quickly or it will oxidise and discolour.

Spaghetti and mussels

Mussels are fairly inexpensive, but very easy and quick to cook and they make a fantastic evening meal. I like to use the cooking liquid to make a creamy sauce to serve with spaghetti or other types of pasta.

500g mussels
200g spaghetti
2 teaspoons vegetable oil
2 teaspoons peeled and
  chopped shallots
50ml dry white wine

300ml double cream
salt and pepper
small bunch of dill, roughly
  chopped
small bunch of parsley,
  roughly chopped

1 tomato, peeled, seeded
  and diced

To serve
Add freshly chopped dill, parsley and diced tomato and serve in warm bowls.

- Scrub the mussels well in cold water and remove the stringy 'beards'. Tap any open mussels and if they do not close up tightly, throw them away.

- Bring a large pan of water to the boil, add some salt and cook the pasta for 8–10 minutes.

- Meanwhile, heat a heavy-bottomed pan and add 1 teaspoon of vegetable oil. Cook 1 teaspoon of the shallots for a few seconds, then add the mussels. Immediately pour in the wine, cover and leave to cook for about 2 minutes or until all the shells are open. Throw away any mussels that do not open. Set the mussels aside to keep warm, and strain and reserve the cooking liquid.

- Next, cook the remaining shallots in the rest of the oil until soft.

- Add the reserved mussel cooking liquid and reduce by half. Season, add the cream and reduce again slightly before adding the cooked mussels.

- By this time the pasta should be ready so strain through a colander and toss with the mussels and cream mixture.

Gravlax
with Swedish sauce (hovmästarsås)

The recipe I use for gravlax is the one used by my wife's Swedish grandfather, Sven. The Swedes are well known for their expertise in curing fish, as the long, harsh winters meant they had to conserve as much produce for the cold months. Raw fish can contain parasites, but these die when heated up or frozen, so freeze the salmon before putting it in the salt mix. It does no harm to the taste or flavour of the fish. Try making the delicious Swedish sauce to go with the gravlax – it will only take you a few minutes!

To serve

Carve the salmon into thin slices and serve with the Swedish sauce.

1 side wild salmon, skin on
1 teaspoon white peppercorns
4 tablespoons sugar
3 tablespoons salt
200g dill, chopped

Swedish gravlax sauce
3 tablespoons Dijon mustard
1 tablespoon sugar
½ teaspoon salt
1 pinch of black pepper

1 tablespoon white wine vinegar
200ml oil
handful of chopped dill

- Freeze the salmon for five days to kill any parasites. Defrost the fish, remove any bones and dry both sides with kitchen paper.

- Crush the peppercorns and mix with the sugar, salt and chopped dill. Place the mix over the flesh of the salmon to cover it completely. Place a tray over the fish, with some weights on top of the tray to press it down, and leave in the fridge for 48 hours. Pour away any excess liquid every 12 hours.

- Remove the fish and wash off the marinade. Dry and wrap well in clingfilm. The gravlax will keep for up to 2 weeks in the fridge or 3 months or more in the freezer.

To make the sauce
- Mix together the mustard, sugar, salt, pepper and vinegar. Start to whisk, adding the oil drop by drop or pouring it in very gently until the sauce thickens – an electric whisk is ideal. Add the chopped dill and an extra sprinkle of newly crushed pepper for added flavour.

Add other flavours to your marinade if you like – such as
coriander seeds or orange zest.

Crispy squid
with marinated red peppers

If you have a deep-fryer in your kitchen this crispy squid will only take a few minutes to prepare. Always be sure to use only fresh oil in the fryer as this will affect the flavour of the end result. The fryer is likely to spit when you add the squid to the hot oil so be careful not to burn yourself.

500ml vegetable oil
250g flour
400g squid
1 teaspoon salt
1 teaspoon black pepper
1 sheet of puff pastry
   (about 21cm x 15cm)
100ml tapenade (see p.45)
fresh basil for garnish

Marinated red peppers
4 large red peppers
6 star anise
100ml olive oil
2 garlic cloves, crushed
2 sprigs of thyme
8 basil leaves, roughly
   chopped
1 teaspoon salt
1 tablespoon sherry
   vinegar

To serve
Place a spoonful of red peppers on each plate. Add a piece of pastry on top, then some more red peppers and top with crispy squid. Serve with the tapenade on the side and sprinkle over a few basil leaves.

To prepare the peppers
• Preheat the oven to 200°C/Gas 6. Arrange the peppers in a deep oven dish with 3 of the star anise and a pinch of salt. Cover tightly with foil and bake for 25–30 minutes, until the peppers are very soft and aromatic. Turn them once or twice. Transfer to a bowl, cover with clingfilm and leave for about 20 minutes. (Covering with clingfilm helps the peppers steam inside their skins and makes it easier to remove the skins.)

• Peel the red peppers and remove the seeds and stalks. Cut the pepper flesh into thin strips. Put the peppers into a bowl and pour in olive oil to cover. Add the remaining star anise, garlic cloves, thyme and basil, salt and sherry vinegar, then stir well. Leave for at least a couple of hours before serving.

Pastry base
• Preheat the oven to 190°C/Gas 5. Lay the puff pastry on a baking tray, prick it all over with a fork and place another baking tray on top – this ensures nice crisp pastry. Bake in the hot oven for about 15 minutes, until golden brown. While the pastry is still hot cut out 4 rectangles measuring about 4cm x 10cm.

Cover any leftover peppers with olive oil and store them in a glass jar. They will keep for up to four weeks.

To cook the crispy squid

• Cut the squid into rings and the tentacles into sections if large. Heat the oil in a deep, heavy-based saucepan until it reaches roughly 200°C. While the oil is heating, put the flour into a bowl, add the squid rings and tentacles and mix gently to coat the squid completely.

• Once the oil has reached 200°C, add the squid in batches and fry until crisp. Drain on kitchen paper and season with salt and pepper.

Skate wings
with grain mustard sauce

Skate is best cooked on the bone as this keeps it lovely and moist. The bones of skate are large so can easily be removed once cooked and you won't find any small bones when eating the fish.

4 pieces of skate wing, about 200g each

300g clams

salt

8–10 heads of purple sprouting broccoli

vegetable oil

50ml white wine

4 tablespoons seasoned flour

Grain mustard sauce

150ml white wine sauce (see p.174)

1 teaspoon Pommery mustard

1 teaspoon chopped chives

To serve

Place a piece of skate on each plate. Add clams and broccoli and some of the grain mustard sauce around the fish.

- Carefully wash the skate wings in plenty of cold water and pat them dry with paper towels or a clean kitchen cloth. Leave in the fridge until needed. Wash and scrub the clams to remove any dirt or grit on their shells.

- Bring a pot of water to the boil. Season it with enough salt to make it taste of the sea and plunge in the broccoli florets. Blanch for 30 seconds, and then transfer them immediately to a bowl of ice water. Take out of the ice water and drain well. Set aside.

- Heat a pan on the stove and add a tablespoon of vegetable oil, the clams and white wine. Cover and cook over a high heat for 3–4 minutes until the clams open, constantly shaking the pan. Once the clams are open, set aside.

- Dust the skate with seasoned flour. Heat a large frying pan with another tablespoon of oil. Once the oil is hot, add the fish and shake gently so that the fish does not stick. Cook for 3–4 minutes on each side. Once the fish is cooked, remove from the pan and serve.

To make the grain mustard sauce

- Heat the white wine sauce. Add the Pommery mustard and chopped chives, then stir well.

Always cook skate the day you buy it, as it doesn't keep well.

Soused herrings

Scotland has a fantastic history of herring fishing and many of the well-known fishing villages along the Scottish coast used to be known as herring ports before developing into coastal holiday resorts. Herring is cheap to buy and works particularly well with mustard, dill and tomato, or marinated with herbs and spices as here.

4 herrings (8 fillets)
3 carrots, peeled and sliced into thin rounds
2 shallots, peeled and thinly sliced

bouquet garni (see p.265)
1 star anise
10 peppercorns
1 tablespoon salt
1 garlic clove, peeled and crushed

1 red onion, peeled and chopped into 3mm thick strips
125ml white wine vinegar

Get yourself a pair of fish tweezers for removing small bones from fish.

- Clean and gut the herrings, remove the heads and pin bones, then fillet. Or ask your fishmonger to do all this for you!

- Put the carrots, shallots, bouquet garni, star anise, peppercorns, salt and garlic in a pan with 1 litre of cold water and bring to the boil. Cover and simmer for 15 minutes. Add the red onion and white wine vinegar and simmer for another 15 minutes. Take off the heat and leave to infuse for 10 minutes.

- Gently roll up the herring fillets and secure each one with a toothpick or skewer. Add the herrings to the stock, which should now be nearly at room temperature, and bring back to a simmer. Poach the fish for 10 minutes, taking care not to let the liquid bubble.

- Leave the herrings to cool in their marinade and then refrigerate, still in the marinade, overnight.

To serve
Serve the herrings, still rolled, with the pickling liquid and vegetables. They're good chilled or at room temperature.

Hare à la royale

This recipe is one of the traditional French dishes I was taught by Pierre Koffmann when I worked with him. It does take time to master, but I find it one of the most satisfying jobs of my kitchen year. In France they hold competitions to determine who can cook the best hare à la royale, which just goes to show that this old classic is still going strong.

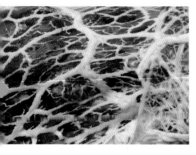

1 hare, 5 or 6kg in weight
1kg crepinette (caul fat), rinsed and drained
200g fresh foie gras

Hare stock
hare carcass
2 carrots, peeled and roughly chopped
1 tablespoon vegetable oil
1 onion, peeled and roughly chopped
1 sprig of thyme

1 bay leaf
½ head of garlic
½ litre veal stock (see p.260)
1 litre red wine

Stuffing
liver, heart, kidneys, blood and lungs of the hare
500g pork fat
100g pork belly
1 onion, chopped
1 garlic clove, chopped

100g unsalted butter
150ml brandy
100ml port
salt and pepper to taste
2 whole eggs

Garnish
5 Brussels sprouts
1 teaspoon vegetable oil
50g pumpkin
50g celeriac
10 sprigs of watercress

To serve
Cover the stuffed hare slices with aluminium foil and warm through in the oven. Place a piece in the middle of each plate with some foie gras on top and add the hare fillets and sauce. Serve with the sautéed vegetables and watercress.

- Bone the hare and separate the legs and the thighs. Carefully bone the thighs and open them out so the meat lies flat. Keep the fillets for the finished dish, and the heart, liver, kidneys, lungs and any blood for the stuffing.

To make the stock
- Chop the hare carcass into small, manageable pieces. Place in a large roasting tray and roast in a hot oven, 200°C/Gas 6, for 45–60 minutes, turning frequently.

- Meanwhile, in a large heavy-bottomed pot over medium heat, cook the carrots in the vegetable oil until they are golden brown. Add the onion and cook for another 5 minutes. Then add the thyme, bay leaf, garlic, veal stock and red wine. Bring to the boil and then turn the heat down low and simmer for 1 hour. Take off the heat and leave to cool for up to 30 minutes. Strain the stock, discarding the vegetables and bones, and set aside.

To make the stuffing
- Mince all the meat together and set aside. In a heavy-bottomed saucepan, cook the onion and garlic in the butter until soft and translucent. Deglaze with the port and brandy. Add seasoning and cook until the liquid has evaporated. Remove the mixture from the pan and spread flat on a large plate to cool. Mix the meat with the cooled onion mix until combined and fold in the eggs. Set aside for later.

Rolling and cooking the hare

* Preheat the oven to 150°C/Gas 2. Lay out the crepinette. Put one opened-out thigh down on the fat first, and then cover with half the stuffing mixture. Lay the foie gras down the middle horizontally and cover with the rest of the stuffing mixture. Place the other thigh on top to cover the stuffing.

* Carefully roll up the mixture in the crepinette and wrap in a piece of muslin. Tie the ends very securely. Place in a large pan and cover with the hare stock. Braise in the oven for 5–6 hours until very tender.

* Then wrap in clingfilm and then leave in the fridge for at least 6 hours. Remove the clingfilm and the muslin and cut into portions.

To make the sauce

* Strain the braising liquid through a fine sieve and reduce in a pan over high heat until slightly thickened.

To cook the hare fillets and foie gras

* Heat the oil in a frying pan. Season the hare fillets and foie gras, add them to the pan and colour over a high heat for 1–2 minutes. Then reduce the heat and cook for a further 3–4 minutes. Remove from pan and leave to rest.

To prepare the garnish

* Blanch the sprouts in boiling water and sauté in a little vegetable oil until golden. Dice the pumpkin and celeriac into 2cm cubes and sauté. Wash the watercress. Feel free to use any other seasonal vegetables that you enjoy.

It's true about 'mad March hares'! Don't cook hare in March as the hares are breeding and the flavour of the meat changes.

Woodcock
with red wine and foie gras sauce

This is a classic winter dish for a special occasion. The method I follow has been used by generations of cooks and must never be changed. It is cooking at its best. Woodcock is an absolute pleasure to prepare. I always use the intestines to create a delicious pâté, and from the bones of the woodcock I make a sauce using a traditional French recipe. I serve the head cut in half in the traditional way, as the brains of the woodcock are a true delicacy.

2 woodcocks, plucked and left whole

2 rashers streaky bacon

1 teaspoon vegetable oil

2 slices of bread for toast, trimmed to 8 x 8cm

30g foie gras

1 teaspoon finely chopped shallot

1 shallot, roughly chopped

salt and pepper

brandy

200ml game red wine sauce (see p.263)

To serve

Warm the woodcock breasts, split head and legs in the oven and serve on top of the toasts. Cover with the sauce.

- Preheat the oven to 200°C/Gas 6. Press the legs and wings of the woodcock together, draw the head round and run the beak through where the legs and wings cross. Lay a piece of bacon on top of each bird and tie it up securely. Brown in a hot pan with a teaspoon of vegetable oil until golden on each side. Transfer to the hot oven and roast for 8–10 minutes.

- Set aside to rest for 10 minutes, breast upwards. Keep the oven on.

- Toast the bread. Remove the stomach, kidneys, heart and liver from the birds – throw away the stomach and intestines. Chop the kidneys, liver and heart very finely and add 10g of the foie gras and the finely chopped shallot. Season with a pinch of salt and pepper. Add a splash of brandy and spread this mixture evenly across the slices of toast.

- Place the toasts in the oven for about 6 minutes.

- Remove the woodcock's head from the neck and split it down the middle exposing the brain – a delicacy. Take the rested breasts and legs off the bird and set aside the carcass for the sauce.

To make the red wine and foie gras sauce

- Chop the carcass and neck bones roughly. Add the rest of the foie gras, the roughly chopped shallot and the red wine sauce. Cook for 10 minutes and then transfer to a blender. Blitz until smooth and pass through a fine sieve.

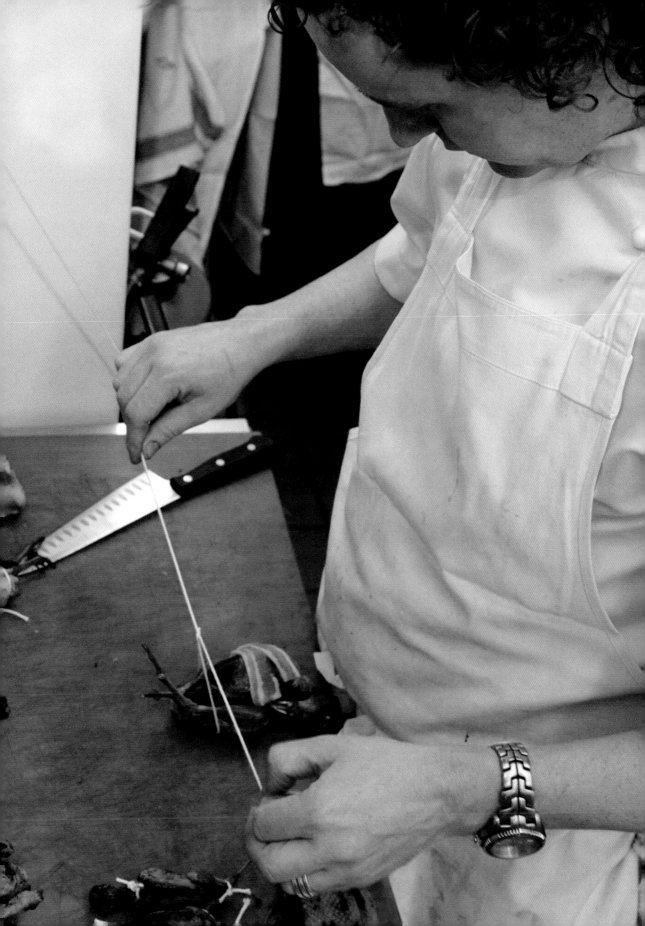

Coq au vin

Serves 4

Mashed potatoes

5 or 6 large baking potatoes
300g rock salt
100g butter
300ml milk
salt and white pepper

Preheat the oven to 200°C/Gas 6. Scrub the potatoes well. Pour the salt onto a baking tray and lay the potatoes on top. Bake for 1½ hours or until the skins are crisp and the flesh soft. While the potatoes are still hot, scoop out the flesh into a bowl. Warm the butter and milk in a pan over medium heat. Start to mash the potatoes and slowly add the milk and butter. Mix until very smooth and glossy, then season to taste. Serve immediately.

To serve

Place some mashed potatoes on each plate and then the coq au vin and sauce. Add some of the mushroom, leek and bacon garnish and serve.

On a really cold winter's night, I can't think of anything I would rather eat than a beautifully cooked coq au vin and some delicious home-made mashed potatoes. Served with a good bottle of red wine, coq au vin is a highlight of my winter cooking.

1 free-range or corn-fed chicken, cut up into legs, breasts, wings and thighs
vegetable oil
4 rashers of bacon, chopped
2 carrots, peeled and chopped into 2cm dice
1 onion, peeled and chopped
3 celery sticks, chopped

1 garlic clove, peeled and crushed
100g seasoned flour
1 bottle red wine
250ml veal stock (see p.260)

Marinade
2 carrots, peeled and chopped
1 onion, peeled and chopped

3 celery sticks, chopped
1 bouquet garni (see p.265)
1 bottle Cabernet Sauvignon

Garnish
200g button mushrooms
4 baby leeks
100g bacon, cut into strips
1 tablespoon olive oil
knob of butter

To marinate the chicken

- Put the chicken in a large bowl with the marinade vegetables and herbs. Cover with wine and leave to marinate for 24 hours. Afterwards, drain the chicken and pat it dry with kitchen towel. Discard the marinade wine and vegetables, as they will have become bitter.

To prepare the chicken

- In a large heavy-bottomed pot, heat a teaspoon of vegetable oil over medium heat and add the bacon, carrots, onion, celery and garlic. Cook until the bacon is crisp and the vegetables golden.

- Meanwhile, heat a tablespoon of vegetable oil in another pan. Dust the chicken pieces with the seasoned flour and sear in the hot oil until golden brown all over. Add the seared chicken to the vegetables and pour in enough red wine to cover. Bring to the boil and then reduce the heat to a simmer. Add the veal stock and bring back to the boil. Again, reduce the heat to a simmer and leave to cook until the chicken is very tender and begins to flake – 45–50 minutes.

- Once the chicken is cooked, remove it from the pan and pass the sauce through a fine sieve. Set the vegetables aside. Pour the sauce back into the pan and reduce until it coats the back of the spoon. Put the chicken and vegetables back in the sauce ready to serve.

To prepare the garnish

- Heat another pan and add the oil and butter. Add the mushrooms, baby leek and the bacon lardons, season and cook for 3–4 minutes.

If you make coq au vin in advance, keep the chicken in the sauce so it stays moist, and warm it up in the sauce before serving.

Roast goose
with apricot stuffing

Serves 6–8

Goose is a great alternative to turkey at Christmas time and I love its intense flavour. With the goose I always serve roast potatoes which are at their best cooked in goose fat. Vacuum-packed chestnuts are fine for the stuffing.

1 goose, about 4–5kg
1 teaspoon salt
white pepper

Apricot stuffing
300g dried apricots
brandy
1.8kg pork mince
1 large onion, peeled and finely chopped
5 sage leaves, chopped

4 sprigs of thyme
1 tablespoon herbes de Provence
2 garlic cloves, peeled and chopped
200g chestnuts, chopped
250g breadcrumbs
2 teaspoons salt
4 eggs

Gravy
1 teaspoon vegetable oil
2 carrots, peeled and chopped
2 onions, peeled and chopped
2 bay leaves
1 small bunch of thyme
500ml red wine
1 litre chicken stock (see p.258)
4 tablespoons plain flour
salt and pepper

To prepare the apricot stuffing
- Put the apricots in a bowl with 2 cups of hot water and a splash of brandy. Leave them to soak for about 10 minutes or until plump. Drain off the excess liquid and chop the apricots roughly.

- In a large bowl, mix the apricots with the pork mince, onion, herbs, garlic, chestnuts, breadcrumbs and salt. Mix until everything is thoroughly combined, then fold in the eggs one at a time. Mix well.

To roast the goose
- Preheat the oven to 190°C/Gas 5. Trim any excess fat from the goose, checking inside as well as out. Season inside and out with salt and white pepper and fill the cavity and neck with the apricot stuffing.

- Put the bird in a large roasting tray and roast in the preheated oven for about 3½ hours, basting regularly. Leave to rest for 10 minutes. Then remove the goose from the roasting tray and set aside in a warm place while you make the gravy.

To make the gravy
- While the goose is roasting, warm the vegetable oil in a large pan over high heat. Add the carrots and cook until caramelised, then add the onions. Cook for another 5 or 6 minutes until soft and add the herbs. Pour in the wine and cook until reduced by two-thirds. Add the chicken stock and reduce again by half. Strain through a fine sieve and set this stock aside for later.

Always keep the fat from roasting a goose
for cooking potatoes.

• When the goose is cooked and resting, pour all but 1 tablespoon of the fat from the roasting tray, keeping all the brown juices. Place the roasting tray on a high heat and stir in the flour with a wooden spoon until you have a smooth brown paste. Slowly pour in the stock you prepared earlier and stir until smooth. Turn down the heat and simmer until the gravy is slightly thickened. Check the seasoning and strain before serving.

To serve
Serve the goose with the stuffing, roast potatoes, seasonal vegetables and gravy. Braised red cabbage (see p.165) also goes well with goose.

Smoked ham hock
with white beans

This recipe takes two days to prepare but I can often get two meals out of it. First we eat the ham hock with the white beans as a tasty supper dish. I keep the leftovers for the next day when I blitz up the white beans to make a delicious soup which we eat with the remaining flakes of the ham hock, and some crunchy croutons (see p.129).

1 large smoked ham hock
250g white beans, soaked
1 teaspoon vegetable oil
2 carrots, peeled and cut
  into 3 large pieces

1 large onion, peeled and
  diced
garlic, peeled and chopped
bouquet garni (see p.265)
1 bunch thyme

bay leaves
1 litre chicken stock
  (see p.258)

The day before
- Start this recipe the day before by soaking the ham in cold water for 24 hours so it's not too salty. Change the water a few times. Soak the beans in cold water overnight.

To cook the ham and beans
- Heat the vegetable oil in a large pan, big enough to hold the ham. Cook the carrots until they are caramelised, then add the onion and garlic and cook for another 6–7 minutes until they are translucent. Add the herbs, ham hock and drained white beans. Pour in the chicken stock. Cover the pan and cook over a medium heat until the beans have absorbed most of the stock and are very soft, and the ham is well cooked and tender. Remove the bouquet garni.

To serve
As this is a rustic dish, serve it as it comes, with some crusty bread to mop up the juices. Give everyone a deep bowl so they can sample the beans as well as the stock and ham.

Remember to soak the beans for at least 12 hours or they will not cook properly.

Confit of duck

You need to start this recipe at least two days ahead so there is plenty of time to cook and cool the confit. The final preparations before serving are then very quick and easy.

4 large duck legs
150g rock salt
1kg duck fat
3 or 4 large potatoes
    (Maris Piper or Rooster)

125ml vegetable oil
salt and pepper
1 small bunch parsley,
    leaves picked off

Preparing the confit

- Place the duck legs in the bottom of a deep bowl and sprinkle with salt. Toss to coat the legs thoroughly, then cover and leave in the fridge overnight. Rinse the salt off with water and pat the duck dry with a cloth.

- Melt the duck fat in a casserole dish into which the legs will fit easily. Add the legs, making sure they are totally submerged in the fat, and cook over a low heat for 2½ –3 hours or until the meat starts to flake away from the bone. Once the duck legs are cooked, remove them carefully with a slotted spoon and chill in the fridge for at least 4 hours.

Preparing the potatoes and crisping the duck

- Peel the potatoes and cut them into 2cm chunks. Bring a large pan of water to the boil, and then cook the potatoes for 3 minutes. Drain and pat dry with a clean kitchen towel.

- Preheat the oven to 200°C/Gas 6. Crisp up the legs by roasting them, skin side down, in a heavy ovenproof pan for 5 minutes. You can also crisp them by placing them under a preheated grill, skin side up.

- While the duck is crisping, heat the vegetable oil in a large non-stick frying pan. Add the potatoes in a single layer, not too tightly packed. (If your pan isn't large enough, fry the potatoes in two smaller batches instead of overcrowding them.) Turn the heat to medium-high and leave the potatoes until they start to brown underneath. Turn them all 2 or 3 times until nicely browned all over – this can take about 7 minutes.

- Lift out with a large slotted spoon and drain on kitchen paper. Sprinkle with sea salt and toss in parsley leaves.

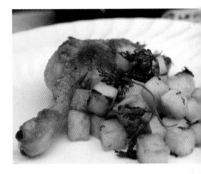

To serve
Place some sautéed potatoes on each plate and top with a crispy duck leg.

You can keep the cooked duck legs in the fridge for 1–2 weeks. Just keep them covered in the duck fat to preserve them and take them out as you need them.

Lambs' tongues
with sweetbread ravioli

There are quite a few stages to this dish so it is best to braise the tongue the day before. Any good butcher will be able to order what you need for this recipe, even if some of the items are only available frozen.

Pasta
500g '00' pasta flour
5 large eggs
1 teaspoon olive oil

Chicken mousse
100g chicken breast
2 egg whites
200ml whipping cream
1 teaspoon curry powder
1 tablespoon chopped tarragon
1 tablespoon chopped chives
salt and pepper

Lambs' sweetbreads
500g lambs' sweetbreads
1 teaspoon vegetable oil
50ml lamb stock (see p.259)

1 tablespoon chopped tarragon
1 tablespoon chopped shallots

Lambs' tongues
1 large onion, peeled and chopped
1 large carrot, peeled and chopped
1 celery stick, chopped
½ leek, chopped
1 bunch of parsley stalks, roughly chopped
½ head of garlic
1 bouquet garni
4 fresh lambs' tongues
salt and pepper

Onion compote
1 tablespoon butter
2 onions, peeled and sliced very thinly
1 pinch salt

Rosemary brochette
4 long sprigs of rosemary
1 lamb's kidney, cut into 8 small pieces
1 garlic clove, peeled and thinly sliced
1 teaspoon vegetable oil

Sauce
100ml lamb stock (see p.259), reduced to 20ml
1 teaspoon grain mustard
1 teaspoon tarragon

To make the pasta dough
- Sieve the flour into a bowl. Break the eggs into a separate bowl, add the olive oil and whisk with a fork. Pour the mixed egg and oil into the flour and mix with a fork until it starts to form a ball. Remove onto a clean working surface and knead for 5–6 minutes until it forms a round of elastic pasta dough. Wrap this in clingfilm and put in the fridge to rest.

Chicken mousse
- Place the chicken and the egg whites into a food processor and pulse until smooth. Add the cream, curry powder and seasoning and pulse until mixed. Remove from the machine into a bowl. Add the herbs and set aside.

- To check the seasoning and consistency of the mousse, drop a teaspoon of the mixture into salted boiling water for 2–3 minutes. Allow it to cool and then taste and add extra seasoning if needed.

Lambs' tongues
with sweetbread ravioli

Lambs' sweetbreads

- Rinse the sweetbreads under cold water and leave them to soak for at least an hour to help remove any impurities.

- Place the rinsed sweetbreads into a pan with cold water, place on the stove and bring to a simmer. This should take no more than 5 minutes. Remove the pan from heat and leave the sweetbreads to cool in the water. When the water is cool enough to put your hand in, remove the sweetbreads and peel off the white skin. Pat dry on kitchen paper.

- In a heavy-bottomed pan, heat the vegetable oil and add the sweetbreads with a good pinch of salt. Cook until they are a deep golden colour. Deglaze the pan with lamb stock and add the tarragon and shallots. Check for seasoning. Leave to cool, then cut the sweetbread into roughly 1 cm dice and fold into the already prepared chicken mousse.

- Fold the cooled sweetbreads into the prepared chicken mousse and leave to rest in the fridge while you roll out the ravioli.

To prepare the lambs' tongues

- Bring a large pot of water to the boil. Season, add the chopped vegetables and herbs and bring back to the boil. Add the tongues and reduce the heat to a simmer. Cook for about 4 hours or until the meat is very tender.

- When the tongues are cooked, lift them out of the pan. While they are still warm, carefully peel off the skin with a knife and set the tongues aside.

To make the ravioli

- Set up your pasta machine. You will only need a quarter of the pasta dough, so keep the rest clingfilmed and refrigerated for another dish. Flour a clean surface and roll the pasta out as thinly as you can with a rolling pin. Then put through the pasta machine until you get to the minimum setting. Cut into two long strips.

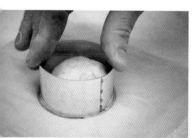

- Take the chicken and sweetbread mousse from the fridge. On half of the rolled out pasta, place four dollops of mousse (the size of a golf ball) at about 6cm intervals. Brush the edges of the pasta with water, then lay the other piece of pasta over the top. Using an upside-down pastry cutter or cup the size of the ravioli, gently form the shape and seal the two sheets of pasta together so they don't separate when cooking.

- To cut out the ravioli, take a pastry cutter half a centimetre larger than the stuffed ravioli and push down to cut. Bring a large pan of water to the boil. Discard the leftover pasta rolled out on the work surface and place the 4 ravioli on a lightly floured dish ready for cooking.

Onion compote
• In a heavy-bottomed pot, heat the butter and begin to sauté the onions. Season, reduce the heat to low and leave the onions to cook very slowly for 45–60 minutes until they are very soft and sweet. Set aside for later.

Rosemary brochettes
• Strip the leaves from the rosemary, leaving just a few attached at the tip of each sprig. Chop the leaves and set them aside to garnish the tongue. To piece together the brochette, thread two pieces of kidney and a slice of garlic onto each rosemary sprig. To cook, heat a frying pan and add the vegetable oil. Sear the brochettes on all sides until they are golden brown – about 2 minutes per side.

Assembling the dish
• When you are ready to serve, bring a large pan of water to a boil, season and plunge in the ravioli. Cook them for 7–8 minutes, then drain. To make the sauce, mix the reduced lamb stock with the mustard and tarragon and warm gently. Trim the tongues and crisp them in a heated, oiled pan until golden brown on both sides. Brush with mustard and sprinkle with the chopped rosemary leaves set aside from the brochettes.

To serve
Serve the ravioli immediately on top of some warmed onion compote and spoon the sauce over the ravioli and around the plate. Add a tongue, a cooked rosemary brochette and some chopped tarragon.

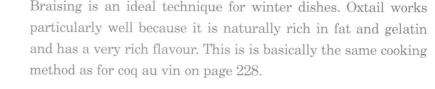

Braised oxtail

Braising is an ideal technique for winter dishes. Oxtail works particularly well because it is naturally rich in fat and gelatin and has a very rich flavour. This is is basically the same cooking method as for coq au vin on page 228.

1kg oxtail, cut into portioned pieces

Marinade
200g carrots, peeled and roughly chopped
200g onion, peeled and roughly chopped
200g celery, roughly chopped
200g leeks, roughly chopped
1 head garlic, cut in half
1 bunch thyme

2 bay leaves
1 litre red wine

Braising mix
seasoned flour
2 tablespoons vegetable oil
1 litre red wine
3 carrots, peeled and chopped
1 onion, peeled and chopped
2 celery sticks, chopped
½ leek, chopped

½ head garlic, cut in half
bouquet garni (see p.265)
1 litre veal stock (see p.260)
salt and pepper

Garnish
1 teaspoon vegetable oil
300g pancetta, cut into 2cm cubes
4 carrots, peeled and cut into large rings
1 bunch flat-leaf parsley, leaves removed from stems and chopped

To serve
Place some bacon and carrot garnish on each plate and top with oxtail. Serve with the reduced braising liquid as the sauce and some crusty baguette to mop up the juices.

Marinate the beef
- Mix the oxtail with the marinade vegetables and herbs. Cover with red wine and leave to marinate for 24 hours. Drain and discard the wine and vegetables.

Preparing the braised oxtail
- Dry the marinated oxtail pieces with kitchen paper and dip them in seasoned flour to coat. Heat a teaspoon of vegetable oil in a large non-stick pan and sear the oxtail to a dark golden brown. Drain off the excess oil and deglaze the pan with the red wine. Set the wine aside for the braising stage.

- Preheat the oven to 180°C/Gas 4. Add the rest of the oil to a large casserole. Sweat the carrots, onion, celery, leek, garlic and bouquet garni. Now add the meat and cover with red wine and the red wine from the deglazing of the oxtail. Bring to the boil, skim, then add seasoning and the veal stock. Cook for 2–3 hours and then check – the meat should be falling off the bone, but cook longer if necessary. Carefully remove the meat from the liquid, strain the braising liquid through a fine sieve. Reduce by half until the sauce is slightly thickened and coats the back of a spoon.

To make the garnish
- Heat the vegetable oil in a large heavy-bottomed pot and add the pancetta. Cook for 6–8 minutes until brown and caramelised. Add the carrots and cook for another 10 minutes or so until they are golden brown and tender. Sprinkle with chopped parsley.

When chopping oxtail, try to find the natural joint. The knife will go through more easily here.

Pork

Pork offers great value and is incredibly versatile, so it is a fantastic ingredient to work with. I especially enjoy experimenting with the many different cuts, especially the loin and shoulders as well as the trotters and head. I often roast, braise or grill pork, but I also combine it with fish and shellfish for so called 'surf-and-turf' dishes. Pork works well throughout the four seasons, but I tend to use pork most in my winter cooking.

To me the interesting thing about pork is comparing breeds to discover great flavours. When shopping for pork I find it frustrating that in many supermarkets the breed of pork is never mentioned. Pork is simply known as pork, whereas beef is clearly labelled with the breed – for example, Aberdeen Angus. I really want to know where the pig was born, when and how it was raised and also what breed it is to understand better what flavour to expect from my pork. I enjoy using pedigree pork, such as Gloucestershire Old Spots and Bramley Old Spot because of the unique flavours of the meat.

During my years of training with Pierre Koffmann, who is well known for his dish of stuffed pig's trotters with morels and veal sweetbread, I developed a liking for pork. Not only did I spend years de-boning pig's trotters in his kitchen, but the experience also taught me how to use and respect the whole animal – you can use all parts of a pig.

My signature dish – boned and rolled pig's head with langoustines and a crispy pig's ear salad – came about from years of working with pork and its various cuts. I enjoy the many hours that go into preparing the dish and the skills and techniques involved in separating the fat from the meat and creating a balance of flavours and texture on the plate. The crispy pig's ear salad, which I serve with the pig's head, is absolutely delicious and brings back memories of eating pork scratchings in my grandparents' local pub in the Midlands as a child. I adore the texture and the crunchiness of the ears.

One of the main influences behind my pig's head dish was my dear nana. I remember her cooking pig's

trotters and pig's head during my childhood. When I worked with Pierre Koffmann, my nana used to love hearing how we prepared pig's trotters, but when I told her that we sold them at £35 a portion at La Tante Claire, she nearly collapsed, as they were given away during the war. She remembered meat rationing, and the main reason for cooking things like trotters and head was because they were cheap and you had to make do with what you could get. My grandfather tells the story of how my nana got caught by the police with half a pig stored under the back seat of her car, as this was over her allowance.

A lot of care and preparation went into the cooking of traditional pork dishes. For brawn, or potted head as it is known in Scotland, the heart, tongue and feet as well as the head were used to create that special dish. My grandfather's job was to put the weights from the scales in the basin and press the potted head after my nana had prepared it and it was a dish that the whole family enjoyed. The trotters that my nana used to make were usually scrubbed, cooked whole and served with cabbage and by rolling the fatty part of the pig's cheeks in breadcrumbs she created an outstanding pig's head dish.

Pork

Today most people are too busy to visit a farmers' market to pick up that special cut of pork, or to experiment with an unusual cut of meat from the butchers. I sometimes hear people telling me they've been unable to get the exact cut they wanted, but instead settled for cuts that were thinner than they would have preferred, or even changed the dishes because they didn't want to ask the butcher for that slightly less common cut. My advice is to go to farmers' markets or talk to your butcher about what you want to cook. Most butchers are glad to have a chat about their meat with anyone who is interested

and many meats can be cut to order on request. It takes years of training for butchers to gain their knowledge and skills and it would be sad to see this trade disappear in favour of mass production and ready-packed produce on our supermarket counters.

One of my pork suppliers is Whitmuir Organics, down in Lamancha in the Scottish Borders. It's important to me to know the background of all the meat I serve at the restaurant and I like to build a close relationship with all my suppliers. Whitmuir Organics has won prices for their fantastic produce, and their meat is delicious and of outstanding quality. I like to know that the farms where I purchase my meat are kept in a good condition and the animals are well looked after, as I am convinced this is reflected in the flavour of the meat.

On this particular farm, as with all of my suppliers, they take great pride in the welfare of the animals. From March to October pigs live in family groups in the woodland and in open ground where they can forage until the frost hits in the late autumn. The pigs work the earth in the way they have done for generations. No artificial fertiliser is allowed, only the natural organic manure from within the cycle. Supplementing the diet with additional grass and clover certainly encourages this natural cycle and enhances the flavours of the meat. This tradition embraces a one-year rotation cycle between pigs and vegetable production allowing pigs one year, and vegetable growing in the same field the following year. This method benefits not only the pork, but also the vegetables – parsnips, turnips, potatoes and carrots. Natural production enhances natural flavours, leading to superb quality.

Bramley Old Spot loin of pork

The Bramley Old Spot pig is a unique cross, bred from the pedigree breeds Gloucestershire Old Spots, Large White and British Landrace. The meat has a distinctive taste and succulent flavour and is well worth trying.

200ml dessert wine
100g golden raisins
1kg loin of pork, cut into 4 portions
1 teaspoon salt
1 teaspoon cracked black pepper
2 teaspoons vegetable oil

150ml pepper sauce (see p.261)
1 teaspoon capers
1 teaspoon chopped chives

Red onion confit
2 red onions
1 tablespoon vegetable oil

Garnish
1 carrot, peeled
1 leek, washed
½ head of celeriac, trimmed
1 tablespoon buttter

To serve
Put some leek, carrot and celeriac on each plate, add some pork on the side and pour over the sauce.

Advance preparation
• Bring the dessert wine to the boil and pour it over the raisins. Leave to macerate for at least a couple of hours, preferably overnight.

To make the red onion confit
• Preheat the oven to 180°C/Gas 4. Cut the onions in half through the root, leaving the skin on. Heat an ovenproof pan and add the oil. When the oil is hot, add the onions, flesh side down, and sear for 4–5 minutes. Place in the oven and cook for 30–35 minutes or until soft when pierced with a knife. Once the onions are cooked, set them aside in a warm place.

To cook the pork
• Preheat the oven to 200°C/Gas 6. Season the pork loin portions with salt and cracked black pepper. Heat a large heavy–bottomed, non-stick pan over a high heat. Add 1 teaspoon of vegetable oil and then the meat. Fry on each side until golden and then transfer to the preheated oven for 5 or 6 minutes or until cooked to medium. Turn the meat once during the cooking time. Remove from the oven and leave to rest for 5 minutes.

Finishing the dish
• Cut the carrot in half lengthways and then in half again. Cut the leek into 4cm pieces and the celeriac into 4 equal pieces. Put the celeriac, carrots and leek in a pan with the butter and half cover with water. Place the pan on a high heat and boil until the water is reduced completely and the butter has caramelised the vegetables. Check they are all cooked and ready to serve.

• Put the prepared pepper sauce in a saucepan and add the capers. Strain the macerated raisins and add them to the pan. Bring the sauce to a simmer and cook for about 5 minutes to allow the flavours to mix. Sprinkle in the chopped chives.

Don't be scared of the fat on pork – that is
where all the flavour is.

Prunes and Armagnac
with prune ice cream

These prunes are a great thing to have in your fridge in the winter months and can be eaten with this delicious prune ice cream or simply with cream. But you need to keep them for at least 3 months before using, so plan ahead and prepare them in the autumn.

1kg pitted prunes	**Prune ice cream**
4 Earl Grey teabags	8 egg yolks
250g caster sugar	180g caster sugar
500ml Armagnac	600ml milk
	200g macerated prunes
	30ml Armagnac

To serve
Serve the prunes with a generous scoop of the ice cream alongside or on top.

The day before
- Bring 1 litre of water to the boil in a large pot. Take the pan off the heat and add the teabags. Allow these to infuse for 2 minutes, then add the prunes and leave them to soak overnight.

To prepare the prunes
- In a small saucepan, bring 2 cups of the prune liquid to the boil and add the sugar to make a sugar syrup. Strain the prunes and put them into a large sealable container such as a Kilner jar and pour in sugar syrup and Armagnac. Seal and keep in the fridge or a cool place for at least 3 months before using.

To make the prune ice cream
- Put the egg yolks and sugar in a bowl and beat until pale and thickened. Pour into a heavy-bottomed pan and warm over a very low heat, stirring constantly. Gradually stir in the hot milk and cook over a low heat, stirring with a wooden spoon until thick enough to coat the back of the spoon. Take off the heat and strain into a large bowl set over ice water. Transfer to an ice cream machine and begin to churn or freeze. Meanwhile, chop the prunes roughly and add them to the ice cream.

- When the ice cream is half frozen, add the Armagnac. Once the ice cream is ready, put it into a plastic container and leave to set for at least 3 to 4 hours before serving.

Any leftover syrup makes a delicious sauce to pour over ice cream.

Plums and barley pudding

The traditional Scottish way of using barley is in soups, but when we were experimenting one day, we came up with the idea of using barley in a dessert. The result was excellent.

Plums	Barley pudding
6 plums, halved and pitted	40g barley, soaked for
peel of 1 lemon	2 hours in cold water
peel of 1 orange	200ml milk
3 tablespoons Demerara	25g sugar
sugar	1 vanilla pod
2 cinnamon sticks	1 leaf of gelatin
300ml red wine	80ml whipped cream
100ml port	

To prepare the plums

- Preheat the oven to 180°C/Gas 4. Put all the ingredients in a large ovenproof dish, making sure to place the plums cut side down. Cover with aluminium foil and bake for 20 minutes or until plums are tender and soft.

To make the barley pudding

- Drain the barley. Put it in a heavy-bottomed saucepan with the milk, sugar and vanilla over a medium heat. Bring to a slow simmer and cook until the barley is soft and has absorbed most of the milk.

- Soften the gelatin in cold water for 3–4 minutes. Squeeze out the excess water and add the gelatin to the barley mixture. Mix thoroughly and set aside to cool to room temperature. Then whip the cream to medium peaks and fold into the barley mixture.

- Pour into a mould and place in the fridge for at least 2 hours or until completely chilled and set.

This cooking technique works equally well with other fruits, such as peaches and apricots.

To serve

Unmould the pudding. Serve the pudding with some plums and spoon over the plum cooking liquid as desired.

Trifle

Trifle must be one of the all-time classic British desserts and perfect for a family gathering. In my family we follow my granny's recipe. She used to love a tipple of sherry and always made sure to add some to her trifle.

Trifle sponge	Custard	Whipped cream
100g plain flour, sifted	100ml milk	500ml whipping cream
125g caster sugar	100ml cream	2 tablespoons crème fraîche
25g cornflour	40g sugar	
4 eggs	1 vanilla pod, split	2 tablespoons caster sugar
25g melted butter	2 egg yolks	chocolate shavings for garnish
1 jar of raspberry jam	1 whole egg	
100ml sherry (optional)		

To make the sponge

- Preheat the oven to 180°C/Gas 4 and line a 23cm cake tin with baking parchment. Mix together the flour, sugar and cornflour in a bowl. In a separate bowl, whisk the eggs and slowly pour in the melted butter. Fold the flour mixture into the whisked eggs and stir until there are no lumps.

- Pour the sponge batter into the lined tin and bake until golden – 25–30 minutes. Leave to cool in the tin for 10–15 minutes and then turn the cake out and cool on a wire rack.

To make the custard

- Bring the milk, cream, sugar and vanilla to a simmer over medium heat. Warm through until the sugar is dissolved and then take off the heat.

- Whisk the yolks and whole egg together in a separate bowl and slowly pour in the milk mixture while still whisking. Pour into a clean pan and place on the heat, stirring constantly until the custard thickens and coats the back of a spoon. Pour the custard into a bowl and leave to cool to room temperature.

Assembling the trifle

- Whip the cream, crème fraîche and sugar together until light and fluffy. Set aside in the fridge until needed.

- Using a breadknife, slice the sponge into 5 layers spreading jam on each layer. Take a medium-sized (3 litre) glass bowl, or some individual glasses or bowls, and begin to layer the ingredients. Start by spreading some custard on the bottom and then add some whipped cream. Then put in a round of sponge, cut to fit the sides of the bowl, and drizzle with sherry if you like. Don't worry if the sponge breaks, as long as it fills the spaces. Top with more custard and cream. Repeat the layers until all the cake, custard and cream is used up, finishing with cream on top. Leave to set in the fridge for 30 minutes before serving.

To serve

Garnish the trifle with some chocolate shavings and slices of fresh fruit.

Surprise your guests by adding a few scoops of ice cream in the middle of the trifle just before serving.

Chocolate tart

This chocolate recipe comes from my pastry chef Sebastian, who was recently a runner-up in the World Chocolate Master finals. It is one of the most popular desserts in our private dining service 'Your Kitchin'.

Sweet pastry
500g flour
100g icing sugar
350g cold unsalted butter, cut into cubes
1 egg

Chocolate filling
450g dark chocolate
300g butter
1 shot Grand Marnier
6 whole eggs
5 egg yolks

60g caster sugar
vanilla
icing sugar for serving

To make the pastry

- Sift the flour and sugar together. Pulse with the butter in a food processor until the mixture resembles breadcrumbs. Mix in the egg and knead gently until the dough clings together. Flatten to a round, wrap in clingfilm and chill in the fridge for 15 minutes.

- Preheat the oven to 200°C/Gas 6. Roll out the pastry to a thickness of about 4mm and line a 23cm pie tin or fluted flan case. Trim the edges and add some parchment paper and 3 cups of baking beans.

- Bake in the preheated oven for 10 minutes, then remove the beans and paper and cook for another 10–12 minutes or until golden.

- While the pastry is still warm brush the inside with beaten egg. This helps to seal the pastry from the tart filling, ensuring a crispy base.

To make the chocolate filling

- Place chocolate, butter and Grand Marnier in a bowl. Cover tightly with clingfilm and place the bowl over a pan of simmering water.

- Allow the chocolate and butter to melt gently until there are no lumps left. Leave to cool.

- Preheat the oven to 150°C/Gas 2. Whisk together the whole eggs, egg yolks, caster sugar and vanilla until tripled in volume. Fold this slowly into the warm chocolate mixture until completely incorporated.

- Pour the chocolate filling into the cooked tart shell and bake for 20–25 minutes. Leave to set at room temperature for 15 minutes, then put the tart into the fridge for at least an hour to finish setting.

To serve

Take the tart out of the fridge about half an hour before you want to eat it – chocolate tastes better when not too cold. Sprinkle with some icing sugar before serving.

Don't try to cut corners by not
allowing your pastry to rest properly – it will shrink.

Almond shortbread
with cranberries and whipped cream

Serves 4

In this recipe I use my almond shortbread with some cranberries and whipped cream as a delicious dessert, but it tastes just as good on its own with a cup of tea in the afternoon. It's so easy to make, too.

Shortbread
150g flour
25g icing sugar
120g butter
75g almonds (skin on), ground
2 tablespoons caster sugar

Cranberries and whipped cream
250ml fresh cranberries
80ml caster sugar
zest of 1 orange
500ml whipping cream

2 tablespoons crème fraîche
1 tablespoon icing sugar
1 sprig of mint

To make the shortbread
- Sieve the flour and the icing sugar together into a bowl. Add the butter and knead by hand until the mixture is light and forms a dough. Add the almonds and continue to knead, then shape the mixture into a rectangular log. Wrap in clingfilm and chill in the fridge for at least 2 hours or until very firm.

- Preheat the oven to 190°C/Gas 5 and line a baking sheet with parchment. Slice the dough into 1cm slices and lay out on the baking sheet. Bake for 12–14 minutes until golden brown. Remove from the oven, sprinkle with caster sugar, then leave the shortbread to cool for 5–10 minutes on the baking tray before removing to a wire rack.

To prepare the cranberries and whipped cream
- Put the cranberries, caster sugar and orange zest into a large saucepan with 150ml of water. Bring to the boil and cook until the cranberries are soft and the liquid has reduced by half.

- Leave to cool. When at room temperature the consistency of the mixture should be thick, like a compote.

- Whip the cream until it forms firm peaks and fold in the crème fraîche and icing sugar. Set aside some of the cranberry mixture for serving and fold the rest into the cream. Leave to set in the fridge.

To serve
Spoon some cranberry mixture onto each plate. Alternate scoops of cranberry cream and shortbread and garnish with mint leaves.

252

Use the finest quality butter for the best shortbread.

Drambuie chocolate mousse

A fine Scottish liqueur, Drambuie is ideal for making special desserts such as this one. The spiced whisky and honey flavour is delicious with the chocolate, but if you don't have any Drambuie, Grand Marnier also works well, adding a touch of orange.

150g dark chocolate
    (70% cocoa)
4 eggs, separated
75g sugar
30g whipping cream
2 teaspoons Drambuie

white chocolate for garnish

- Break up the chocolate and put it into a bowl. Bring a saucepan of water to simmering point, then set the bowl over the pan of water until the chocolate melts. Set aside. Put the egg yolks and 25g of the sugar in another bowl, set this over the pan of water and whisk until the mixture starts to form ribbons and coats the back of a spoon. Set aside.

- Whisk the egg whites and the remaining 50g of sugar to stiff peaks. In another bowl, whisk the cream to soft peaks.

- Mix the melted chocolate into the egg yolks until smooth and add the Drambuie. Gently fold in the egg whites and then the cream. Pour the chocolate mousse into 4 glasses and leave to set for 2–3 hours in the fridge.

To serve

Serve with some shavings of white chocolate on top – use a potato peeler to make the shavings.

Brioche and butter pudding

Serves 4

Brioche can be bought in any good bakery and kept in the freezer if you can't use it right away. Its high butter content makes it ideal for bread and butter pudding and the redcurrant jelly gives that extra twist of flavour.

50g raisins	100g redcurrant jelly
50ml rum	400ml whipping cream
10 slices brioche	25g sugar
25g butter	3 free-range eggs
2 teaspoons cinnamon	

• Soak the raisins overnight, or for about 10 hours, in the rum. Cut the brioche into thin slices, remove the crusts and cut into triangles. Grease a pie dish with butter and arrange some brioche slices in the bottom of the dish. Sprinkle with cinnamon and raisins and spoon in half the redcurrant jelly. Repeat the process until you have used all the brioche slices.

• Pour the whipping cream into a saucepan, add the sugar and warm until all the sugar has dissolved. Crack the eggs into a bowl and whisk them until pale. Add the cream and strain the custard through a sieve into a bowl while still hot.

• Pour the custard over the brioche and leave to rest for 20 minutes to allow the custard to soak into the brioche. Preheat the oven to 180°C/Gas 4 and bake the pudding for 35–40 minutes.

To serve
Serve warm with vanilla ice cream or cream.

Stollen

I always eat lots of this stollen cake during December. If you could put a taste to Christmas, I think this would be it.

100ml milk	1 egg	5ml dark rum
25g dried yeast	75g cut mixed peel	30g flaked almonds
300g plain flour	zest of ½ lemon	100g butter
50g icing sugar	1 pinch of salt	300g raisins
		extra butter and caster sugar

- Heat the milk to luke-warm and dissolve the dried yeast. Put all the remaining ingredients, except the butter and raisins, into a bowl with the milk and yeast and mix by hand to make a dough. Cover with a damp cloth and leave to rest in a warm place for 30 minutes

- Add the butter and raisins and knead them into the dough, then leave to rest for a further 30 minutes. Once rested, knock back and divide the dough into 2 pieces. Cover with a damp cloth and leave to rest again for 20–30 minutes. Roll out each piece of dough to about the thickness of your finger. Make two dips in the dough with the rolling pin, then fold the dough into the middle and back onto itself (see pictures). Repeat with the other piece of dough. Leave the loaves to rest for another 15 minutes with a damp cloth over them.

- Preheat the oven to 180°C/Gas 4. Place the stollen in the centre of the oven and bake for 40 minutes. Remove from the oven and leave to cool for 10 minutes. Remove any burnt raisins you can see, then brush the stollen with butter and toss in caster sugar. Leave for about 1 hour to cool completely, then wrap in clingfilm and store in a cool place for up to 4 weeks.

To serve

Dust with icing sugar, slice and arrange on a plate.

Basic recipes

Here are my versions of some basic stocks, sauces and other essentials that you will need for a number of the recipes in this book. These are all useful recipes to know how to make – stocks, in particular, are easy to prepare and make all the difference to the flavour of your soups and other dishes. Stocks can be kept in the fridge for 2–3 days, but they all freeze well and can be stored in the freezer for 3–4 months.

Chicken stock

Makes 2 litres

2.5kg raw chicken carcasses
½ head celery, roughly chopped
1 large leek, white part only, roughly chopped
1 large onion, roughly chopped

4 sprigs of fresh thyme
4 sprigs of parsley
2 bay leaves
12 white peppercorns, crushed
salt

- Remove any excess fat from the chicken carcasses, chop them roughly and place in a large saucepan. Cover with 3.5 litres of cold water, bring to the boil and then reduce the heat. Let the stock simmer for 30 minutes, skimming frequently to remove the impurities that float to the surface.

- Add the chopped vegetables, herbs, crushed white peppercorns and a large pinch of salt and cook for a further 1½ hours. Continue to skim the stock frequently and adjust the seasoning if necessary.

- Pass the chicken stock through a fine sieve into a stainless steel container and then refrigerate. Any fat will solidify and rise to the surface. Remove the fat before using the stock.

Vegetable stock

Makes 1 litre

3 celery sticks, roughly chopped
2 leeks, roughly chopped
2 carrots, peeled and roughly chopped
1 onion, peeled and roughly chopped
2 garlic cloves, peeled and chopped

500ml dry white wine
2 whole star anise
1 bouquet garni (see p.265)
1 scant teaspoon coarse salt
pepper

- Pour 1.5 litres of water into a large saucepan, add all the ingredients and bring to the boil. Lower the heat and simmer gently for 1 hour, uncovered, skimming any foam from the surface every 10 minutes. Remove the pan from the heat and leave to infuse for 30 minutes.

- Pour the stock into a fine sieve and let it drip through naturally. Do not force or press the vegetables, as this will discolour the stock.

Fish stock

Makes 1 litre

2kg fresh white fish bones, such as turbot, sea bass or John Dory
1 medium onion, roughly chopped
1 medium leek, white part only, roughly chopped
1 celery stick, roughly chopped
1 small fennel bulb, roughly chopped
2 garlic cloves, crushed
50ml olive oil
100ml Noilly Prat
200ml dry white wine
1 bay leaf
12 white peppercorns, crushed
2 sprigs fresh thyme
2 sprigs fresh parsley

• Chop the fish bones into small pieces and wash them under cold running water to remove all traces of blood. When the water runs clear, drain the bones in a colander. Wash the chopped vegetables in cold water and drain.

• Warm the olive oil in a heavy-bottomed saucepan over a medium heat. Add the onion, leek, celery, fennel and garlic and sweat without colouring for 5 minutes. Add the fish bones and continue to sweat for a further 3 minutes without colouring. Add the Noilly Prat and white wine and cook until the alcohol has evaporated. Pour 2 litres of cold water over the bones and bring to the boil. Reduce the heat to a simmer and remove any scum that floats to the surface.

• When the stock is clear and the fish bones have settled on the bottom, add the bay leaf, peppercorns, thyme and parsley and cook the stock for a further 15 minutes. Remove the stock from the heat and pass through a fine sieve into a clean saucepan. Discard the bones and vegetables.

• Put the stock back onto the heat and reduce by half to concentrate the flavour. Pass the reduced stock through a fine sieve into a stainless steel container and refrigerate. Any fat will solidify and rise to the surface. Remove the fat before using the stock. The fish stock will keep for 2 days in the fridge.

Lamb stock

Makes 1 litre

2.5kg lamb bones, chopped
5 carrots, chopped
1 onion, chopped
1 fennel bulb, chopped
1 handful thyme
1 head of garlic, cut in half
½ red pepper, chopped
1 teaspoon ground cumin
2 tablespoons olive oil
100ml tomato purée
100ml white wine

• Preheat the oven to 200°C/Gas 6. Put the lamb bones in a roasting tray with half the oil. Roast for 20–25 minutes until golden brown.

• Add the rest of the oil to a heavy-bottomed pan and sweat the carrots, onion, fennel, thyme and garlic on top of the stove for a good 8–10 minutes. Add the red pepper and the cumin and cook for another 3–4 minutes. Add the tomato purée and cook for a further 2–3 minutes.

• Pour the white wine into the pan and add the roasted lamb bones. Cover with about 2 litres of water, bring to the boil and skim. Cook for 3–4 minutes, then pass through a fine sieve. Pour the stock back in the pan and boil until reduced by half.

Basic recipes

Veal stock

Makes 2 litres

3kg fresh veal bones
30ml vegetable oil
1 onion, roughly chopped
1 carrot, peeled and
  roughly chopped
1 celery stick, roughly
  chopped
1 leek, white part only,
  roughly chopped

½ head garlic
25g tomato paste
2 bay leaves
1 bunch thyme
1 teaspoon black
  peppercorns

- Preheat the oven to 200°C/Gas 6. Coat the bones in half the oil and roast in the hot oven until brown, turning the bones frequently so they colour evenly.

- Drain the bones and place them in a heavy-bottomed pot and cover with 4 litres of cold water – set the roasting pan aside for later. Bring the pot of bones to the boil, then reduce the heat to a simmer and cook for 30 minutes. Skim regularly to remove the impurities that float to the surface.

- Pour the remaining oil into the pan in which the bones were roasted. Add the vegetables and return to the oven to cook for 20 minutes until caramelised. Stir the vegetables and loosen the sediment left behind by the bones. Mix the tomato paste into the vegetables, add the bay leaves, thyme and peppercorns and continue to cook for another 10 minutes.

- Add the vegetables to the stock and cook for a further 8–10 hours, occasionally topping up with water to ensure the bones stay covered. Skim frequently. Pass the stock through a coarse sieve to remove the bones and vegetables. Then pass the stock through a fine sieve into a pan and boil to reduce the liquid by half. Cool in a clean container and refrigerate. Any fat will solidify and rise to the surface. Remove the fat before using the stock.

Celeriac purée

Makes 500ml

1 whole celeriac
30g unsalted butter
200ml whipping cream

200ml milk
juice of ½ lemon
salt

- Peel the celeriac and chop into 2cm dice. In a heavy-bottomed pan, sweat the celeriac with the butter and a pinch of salt for 4–5 minutes with the lid on. Add the cream, milk and lemon juice and cook for 30–40 minutes until completely soft. Take care – if the liquid reduces too fast, you will have to add more.

- Once the celeriac is cooked, blend until completely smooth, season and set aside to cool. The purée can be kept in the fridge for 2–3 days.

Beetroot purée

Makes 200ml

4 cooked beetroot
25ml sherry vinegar
salt

- In food blender, blitz the beetroot for 2 minutes until completely puréed. Add the vinegar and salt to taste. Place in a very fine sieve or muslin cloth and leave to drip for 2–3 hours until left with only the purée. Keep refrigerated until ready to serve.

Tomato concasse

Makes 100ml

20 tomatoes
5 garlic cloves, peeled

2 sprigs thyme
salt and pepper

- Put a large pan of water on to boil and prepare a bowl of iced water. Cut a cross on the top of each tomato. Plunge the tomatoes into boiling water for 20 seconds and then put them straight into the iced water. Remove from water and peel the skins from the tomatoes.

- Cut the tomatoes into quarters and remove the seeds. Put into a heavy-bottomed pan with the garlic and thyme. Cook over a gentle heat for 1½ hours or until the tomatoes have reduced to one third their original volume. Season to taste with salt and pepper.

Béchamel sauce

Makes 800ml

60g butter
60g flour

1 litre milk
salt

- In a medium saucepan, melt the butter gently, taking care not to let it brown. Add the flour, all at once, and whisk to mix it with the butter. Make sure there are no lumps. Stir continuously for 2–3 minutes over a low heat. The mixture should whiten, foam and look as if it is boiling but never bubble. Remove the saucepan from the heat and allow it to cool.

- Bring the milk to the boil, pour it over the cooled mixture and whisk to make a smooth, lump-free sauce. Put it back on the stove, bring it to a bubble and cook for 10 minutes at most, stirring and maintaining a very gentle simmer. Season with a pinch of salt. The cooked béchamel sauce can then be passed through a fine strainer to remove any lumps that may have formed.

Pepper sauce

Makes 250ml

50g pancetta, diced
1 teaspoon vegetable oil
6 shallots, diced
large sprig of thyme
20 cracked peppercorns

1 tablespoon white wine vinegar
100ml brandy
300ml veal stock (see p.260)

- In a heavy-bottomed pan, cook the pancetta with the oil until caramelised (about 45 minutes). Add the diced shallots, thyme and crushed peppercorns and sweat on a low to medium heat for a further 4–5 minutes. Add the vinegar and reduce until dry. Add the brandy and reduce until dry.

- Pour in the veal stock and cook for 45–55 minutes. Pass through a sieve before serving.

Venison sauce

Makes 500ml

1kg venison carcass, chopped
2 tablespoons olive oil
250g venison trimmings
50g shallots
50g carrots
25g celery

1 teaspoon peppercorns, crushed
150ml port
150ml red wine
1.5 litres chicken stock (see p.258)

- Heat a heavy-bottomed pan with the oil. Add the venison bones and trimmings and brown them for about 10 minutes until golden and caramelised.

- Add the vegetables and peppercorns to the pan and sweat for a further 8–10 minutes on a low to medium heat. Add the port and the red wine and reduce until the liquid has evaporated. Pour in the chicken stock and cook for 45 minutes to 1 hour until the stock is reduced by half and has a consistency that coats the back of a spoon. Pass through a sieve and it is ready to serve.

Basic recipes

Langoustine bisque

Makes 400ml

2 tablespoons vegetable oil
1kg langoustine heads
3 carrots, peeled and chopped
3 shallots, peeled and chopped
2 celery sticks, chopped
5 fresh tomatoes, chopped

1 handful tarragon
50g tomato paste
100ml brandy
100ml white wine
500ml whipping cream
salt and pepper

- Preheat the oven to 200°C/Gas 6. Heat half the oil in a roasting tray until smoking and then add the langoustine heads. Sweat for 2–3 minutes, then place in the oven for 8–10 minutes. Remove the langoustines from the oven and gently smash the heads with a rolling pin.

- Meanwhile, add the rest of the oil to a heavy-bottomed pan and sweat the carrots, shallots and celery for 5–6 minutes. Do not let them brown. Add the tomatoes, the tarragon and the tomato paste and sweat for a further 2–3 minutes.

- Add the smashed langoustine heads and mix well. Deglaze the pan with the brandy and white wine and reduce until dry. Add the cream and bring to the boil, then skim the surface and leave to simmer gently for 20–25 minutes. Remove from the heat and leave to infuse for 15 minutes. Pass through a fine sieve, then pour back into the pan and reduce by half. Season to taste.

Game red wine sauce

Makes 600ml

1 teaspoon vegetable oil
1kg game bones, chopped into roughly 2 cm dice
4 shallots, chopped
1 bay leaf

small handful of thyme
6 peppercorns, crushed
500ml red wine
300ml veal stock (see p.260)
salt and pepper

- Heat the oil in a heavy-bottomed pan, add the game bones and caramelise for 6–8 minutes until golden brown. Add the shallots, bay leaf, thyme and peppercorns and cover with the red wine. Bring to the boil and skim. Add the veal stock and cook for 1½–2 hours over a medium heat.

- Pass the sauce through a fine sieve, then pour back in the pan and reduce by half. Season to taste.

Sauce Gribiche

Makes 300ml

6 free-range eggs
1 teaspoon Dijon mustard
25ml white wine vinegar
250ml vegetable oil
1 tablespoon chopped capers

1 tablespoon chopped gherkins
1 tablespoon chopped parsley
salt

- To hard boil the eggs, cook in boiling water for 8–10 minutes. Cool in running cold water and peel. Chop the eggs into fine dice and set aside.

- In a separate bowl, whisk together the mustard and the vinegar and slowly pour in the vegetable oil, whisking all the time. Add the chopped capers, gherkins, parsley and salt. Refrigerate until ready to use. The sauce keeps for 2–3 days in the fridge.

Basic recipes

Vegetable crisps

1 beetroot	1 salsify
1 celeriac	2 litres vegetable oil
1 Jerusalem artichoke	100g flour
1 parsnip	salt

- Preheat the oil in a large pan or deep fryer to 160–170°C. Peel all the vegetables and cut them into thin slices on a mandolin. (For the salsify, just wash off the dirt and cut into strips with a vegetable peeler.) Dust gently with flour and place them in the hot oil. Cook for 2–3 minutes, mixing them with a fork, until crispy. Remove from the oil and drain on kitchen paper. Add salt and serve.

Melba toast

½ loaf of sourdough bread
  (one day old)
3 tablespoons olive oil

- Preheat the oven to 150°C/Gas 2. Cut the loaf into very thin slices – about 2mm (day-old bread is easier to slice thinly than fresh). Place the sliced bread on baking tray, drizzle with olive oil, then cover with another baking tray. Bake for 4–5 minutes until golden brown and crispy. Cool and serve. The toast keeps well in an airtight container.

Clarified butter

150g butter

- Gently melt the butter in a pan over the lowest possible temperature. The water and milk will separate and go to the bottom and the pure butter will be on top. Gently pour through a strainer and discard the white solids.

Preserved lemons

Makes one large jar

12 lemons	**Syrup**
220g salt	1kg sugar
150g sugar	

- To make the syrup, boil the sugar with 2 litres of water. Set aside to cool.

- Cut the lemons into four, but do not cut all the way through, so the pieces remain attached. Mix the salt and 150g sugar. Carefully open out the lemons and add a good pinch of the salt and sugar mix. Close the lemons up again and place them into a large, airtight jar, making sure they are tightly packed. Add the remaining salt and sugar and cover with the cooled syrup.

- Seal the jar and leave for three months before using the lemons.

Orange reduction

Makes 100ml

½ vanilla pod
3 oranges
80g caster sugar

- Cut the vanilla pod lengthways and scrap out the seeds. Grate the outer peel of one orange. Cut all 3 oranges in half and squeeze the juice.

- Place the juice in a saucepan with the vanilla seeds, pod and grated peel. Add 50ml water and the sugar and bring to boil. Reduce the heat and keep simmering until the liquid is reduced by about half. The consistency should be like syrup. Use while still warm.

Custard

Makes 500ml

500ml milk	4 egg yolks
70ml single cream	25g caster sugar
1 vanilla pod, split lengthwise	2 teaspoons cornflour

- Add the milk, single cream and vanilla pod to a heavy-bottomed pan and set over medium heat.

- Bring to a simmer and then remove from the heat and set aside so the vanilla can infuse for 10 minutes. Remove the vanilla pod.

- Whisk the egg yolks, sugar and cornflour together in a bowl. Slowly pour in the milk and cream mixture while still whisking and continue until it is completely incorporated. Pour back into the heavy-bottomed pan, place over the heat and stir until the custard thickens. Pass through a sieve. Serve warm or pour the custard into an airtight container and keep in the fridge until ready to serve.

Biscuit tuiles

50g butter, room temperature	1 egg white
50g icing sugar	30g plain flour, sifted

- Preheat the oven to 200°C/Gas 6. Combine all the ingredients in a bowl and mix with a wooden spoon until smooth. Line an oven tray with baking parchment.

- Drop tablespoons of the mixture onto the baking parchment and spread to the desired shape. Be sure to leave space between each one. Bake in the middle of the oven for 10 minutes until golden brown. Set them aside to cool until ready to serve. If you want to shape the tuiles, you must do this while they are still warm.

Bouquet garni

2 leek leaves	1 bay leaf
1 handful of parsley	butcher's string
1 handful of thyme	

- Wash the leek leaves in cold water to remove the soil. Place one leaf down flat, put the herbs and bay leaf on top and cover with the other leek leaf. Tie with string and use as needed.

Index

Index

Index

Acknowledgments

Michael Dover and Susan Haynes at Weidenfeld & Nicolson – thank you for this opportunity.

Lucie Stericker and Rich Carr for the design.

Jinny Johnson for your patience and your can-do attitude.

Marc Millar for outstanding photography and for sharing our passion and vision for this book.

Philippe Nublat, Dominic Jack, Sebastian Kobelt and the entire team at The Kitchin.

Jenny Ingram and the girls at Stripe Communications.

Pierre Koffmann, the legend!

Le Creuset, Livingston.

Mum and Dad for your endless support – I love you both!

Kasper, the joy of our lives.

Michaela – thank you for all your hard work and for putting my words down on paper. Without you none of this would have happened. I love you more than words can say!

A PHOENIX PAPERBACK

First published in Great Britain in 2009
by Weidenfeld & Nicolson
This paperback edition published in 2011
by Phoenix,
an imprint of Orion Books Ltd,
Orion House, 5 Upper St Martin's Lane,
London WC2H 9EA

An Hachette UK company

10 9 8 7 6 5 4 3 2 1

Text Copyright © Tom and Michaela Kitchin 2009
Design and layout copyright © Weidenfeld & Nicolson 2009

Photography by Marc Millar
www.marcmillarphotography.com

Design www.carrstudio.co.uk
Edited by Jinny Johnson
Proofread by Susan Haynes
Index by Elizabeth Wiggans

A CIP catalogue record for this book
is available from the British Library.

ISBN 978-0-7538-2656-0

Printed and bound in China

The Orion Publishing Group's policy is to use papers that are natural, renewable and recyclable products and made from wood grown in sustainable forests. The logging and manufacturing processes are expected to conform to the environmental regulations of the country of origin.

www.orionbooks.co.uk